TREASURED TRIBES

"Christie Ruffino simply embodies everything a leader should be: wise, humble, giving, encouraging, an ongoing learner, a mentor, and a person who provides extraordinary value to the lives of everyone she touches. In Treasured Tribes she taps into the lessons she has learned and shares with us how we can also accomplish that which we desire; more than we might previously have thought possible. Study this book, apply her wisdom, and watch how you begin to greatly increase and expand the value you provide to others. As a result, watch your peace of mind, fulfillment, income, and general sense of happiness greatly increase. Oh, and for the record…I would belong to ANY tribe that Christie is leading!"

—Bob Burg
Co-Author of *The Go-Giver*
www.Burg.com

"I love this latest book from Christie Ruffino. Whether you are new to the world of networking or a consummate pro, there is something you can learn from Treasured Tribes! I love that it addresses and blasts through common networking presumptions, inviting the reader to dive a little deeper as to their motivations for engaging in this common business growth practice. Christie also deep dives into the importance of different types of networking, from the typical meet and greet, to the Mastermind level event, to building a Treasured Tribe. She then provides an action plan to help the reader get more out of their experience. This really is a fully comprehensive book about Intentional Networking, allowing you to create and even exceed your engagement and business expectations."

—Viveka VonRosen
Author of *LinkedIn Marketing: An Hour a Day*
www.LinkedIntoBusiness.com

"A great resource for those who want to have a solid understanding of effective networking, from beginners to more experienced entrepreneurs. Author Christie Ruffino gives great examples of what networking is and is not. Not only does Christie show what not to do, she shares examples of how to get the most out of every networking opportunity available. An easy read. Fast, to the point and entertaining. A nice addition to any woman's professional book library."

—Kathleen Gage
Online Marketing Strategist and Product Creation Specialist
www.PowerUpForProfits.com

"With great transparency and authenticity, Christie shares her life experiences and professional knowledge to guide you to your ideal referral networking experience. This book artfully hits on every point you need to build a powerful tribe network, no matter your personality type or confidence level. You will learn how draw upon your dreams—your WHY—to demystify the world of networking and the success it can bring."

—Marla Tabaka
International Success Coach, Leading Author, Inc. Magazine on-line
www.MarlaTabaka.com

"Christie Ruffino, in her latest book Treasured Tribes, writes about the importance of having Networking Tribes, and she touches on something I have not seen in any other books that talk about "networking." In Chapter 3, she does an in-depth analysis of Introverts and Extroverts and the classic characteristics of each. After discussing each personality type, she goes on to provide Action Plans for each. As she points out, it is important to understand that people look at things and react to things in different ways, based on their personalities. It is the balance of introverts and extroverts working off each other's strength that makes the tribe successful."

—James E. Thompson, JD
Author of *Why Lawyers Fail to Get Referrals*
www.LawyersMarketingResource.com

"Networking is more than just handing out business cards. It's about building relationships... building your tribe! Christie Ruffino shares practical tips and strategies for building lifelong clients and friends in her book, Treasured Tribes. If you're looking to grow your business, then this book is a must-read!"

—Michelle Prince
Best-Selling Author and Self-Publishing Expert
www.MichellePrince.com

"Christie Ruffino has written the ultimate guide to networking... with a heart. You will learn that powerful and purpose-filled networking, and being part of a "treasured tribe," will add much more than new business to your life; it will bring lifelong friends. If you are searching for a better strategy, and certainly better results, I highly recommend that this book become part of one's library. Embrace and implement the simple strategies and get the most out of your networking experiences."

—Johnna Parr
Author of *When the Dream is Big Enough* and Global Leader at "Vi"
www.MattandJohnnaParr.com

"This is not just another networking book. In Treasured Tribes, Christie Ruffino actually goes into more than just how to network. Christie breaks down networking into a plan you can execute going into networking for your personality type and networking with your goals in mind. This new book is an amazing compilation of how to network the right way to create a huge and dynamic referral network using a tribe of trusted partners within your community."

—Tiffany Hinton
Author and Speaker
www.GFMomCertified.com

"Treasured Tribes is a must-read book. Christie Ruffino has done a great job of telling us what a 'Treasured Tribe' is and what it is not. If you don't know, your networking will never have the impact on your business. So many people are looking for the 'golden egg' (what's in it for them) when they should be looking for the 'golden goose' (strong business relationships)."

—Jean Kuhn
Author of *F*Ups, Franchisee Screw-Ups That Can Cost You Thousands*
www.JeanKuhn.com

"Everything you will do in life will be with people, for people and by people. This practical book gives you all the tools, resources and how-to's to make meaningful connections with others as a way to achieve the success you desire."

—Jacqueline Camacho-Ruiz
Award-Winning Author
www.JackieCamacho.com

"I really enjoyed reading about the lessons learned on the author's networking journey. One of the points that resonated with me is the importance of having a mindset of serving others versus being a 'taker.' This was a quick read and will be a much-used reference for the future."

—Courtney Powell
Lifestyle Strategist, Speaker and Author
www.CourtneyPowellonPurpose.com

"Christie opened up my eyes to the things I need to do so that I may better network. I thought I was doing pretty good, but I learned by reading her book that I need to be more specific with my goals and take certain steps. You will not get to your destination if you do not put the address into your GPS first. I was networking so hard that I did not have time to follow up with the people who expressed interest in working with me. Consequently, I wasted their time and mine. I wish I would have read her book years ago."

—Amazon Customer

TREASURED
TRIBES

ALSO BY CHRISTIE RUFFINO

TREASURED TRIBES

The Smart Entrepreneur's Guide to Building
a 5-Star Network of Prospects, Clients
and Brand Advocates.

Christie Ruffino

DPWN Publishing

Front cover and book design by DPWN Publishing

Published by DPWN Publishing
A division of the Dynamic Professional Women's Network, Inc.
1879 N. Neltnor Blvd. #316, West Chicago, IL 60185
www.OurDPWN.com

For permission requests, speaking inquiries and bulk order purchase options, email info@ChristieRuffino.com

dpwn
PUBLISHING

Printed in the United States of America

ISBN 978-1-939794-04-8

3rd Edition

To my mom, who taught me to never give up.

To my dad, who taught me I could do anything I set my mind to do.

To the world's best step-dad, who taught me patience and unconditional love.

To my kids: "I love you to infinity and beyond!" (All of you)

And to my grandkids, whom I love more than I ever thought possible.

Hugs and forever-love!

Our lives are a series of circumstances that send us traveling down the dirt roads of life. Most of the time we do the best we can to manage every experience, both good and bad. We move through them without much thought. **We Live.**

Sometimes we travel down a road that brings us face-to-face with a terrible tragedy, regardless of our input. We navigate through, one step at a time, and move on. **We Cope.**

Other times, our road will bring us to times of monumental pain. We reflect and modify our future behaviors in order to continue on a better journey. **We Learn.**

Eventually, as we travel down these roads, we face more new opportunities and challenges. We become better equipped to navigate through life because of our accumulated experiential knowledge. **We Grow.**

Sometimes we are fortunate enough to recognize one specific event, or a series of events, that have brought us to a great place in life. We reach a place where we truly know we are living the life God created us to live, and where we are following our passion and making a real difference in the world. **We Thrive.**

— ***Christie Ruffino***

CONTENTS

PREFACE

When I first met Claire, she could barely make eye contact with me or anyone else in the room. Her response to those who greeted her was a quick hello and then an even quicker withdrawal, as she inched her way to a safe place at the table to sit and wait for the meeting to start.

It was June 2007, and we were building another new chapter of the Dynamic Professional Women's Network, Inc. in St. Charles, Illinois. The meeting started out strong, with a room full of ladies who came to learn about this new women's organization that had been making a buzz in the Chicagoland suburbs.

Somehow Claire had found out about the group. She was building a business with a network marketing company of nutritional products. I don't remember the exact details, but one of her children had started taking the products to treat a health condition and had a complete turn-around. To say that Claire was excited to share those amazing results with the world was an understatement. She was elated!

But even with all her heartfelt motivation, when it came time to give her 60-second infomercial, she bombed painfully. She didn't stand up, she was very quiet, and she spoke her words down towards the table. She was just too nervous and shy to be able to showcase her business effectively.

Over time Claire gained confidence and developed better speaking skills. She learned how to share her story in a way that created a desire in others to improve their health just as she and her family had. She developed an unshakable confidence about her business. She gained solid leadership skills, and eventually built a large team within that company. She also earned the respect of her fellow chapter members and eventually, became the Chapter Director of that group.

This is just one of many success stories from women who've developed personally within our DPWN community. There have been countless others.

Over the years, thousands of women have been actively involved in our organization in their effort to gain more clients and grow their businesses. They join for professional reasons, yet they tend to stay for personal reasons. Most of our members remain with us for an avarage of 3-5 years, however a few of them have stayed for much longer. Eventually they either transition out of networking completely or they focus their networking efforts in a different way. Their need to follow the DPWN networking system became less relevant as their business scales and their focus shifts. I like to say that they "outgrew" us. Those are the bittersweet success stories.

We would love for every woman who becomes a DPWN sister to stay with us forever; but if that were to happen, we would not be an effective business tool for them.

We WANT our members to outgrow us.

We WANT them to be uber-successful.

And we WANT them to know that even when they are no longer actively involved, they will forever remain a part of our DPWN family.

Many of the stories to come are from women such as these. Women who have stayed connected with our community in some way, or with one or more of our members. Since the core of our success is built on relationship-building, our members make many valuable connections that will last a lifetime.

Our women go through life together while they build their businesses. Along the way they get to know each other's families, hobbies, and health struggles, as well as their business goals and challenges. They create partnerships to support each other as business mentors, accountability partners, and marketing teams; and most importantly, as an extended sales force for each other. They create bonds together, forging an organic connection, so that they are motivated to invest in each other.

In a busy, fast-paced world, our amazing women make each other a priority. They never have to feel as if they're out there doing anything alone.

Our women ROCK!

Our community ROCKS!!

Our leadership team ROCKS!!!

And you ROCK!!!!

If you're reading this preface, you are actually reading a revised version of my original Treasured Tribes book. My goal for republishing this book is three-fold.

One

First, when I originally released this book, I was rushing to complete and release it at our first Dynamic Women's Conference back in 2015. I had been sporadically working on it for over four years, but I wanted to finish and debut it at that event. My plan was to draw on the audience's support in an effort to make the book reach the #1 position in an Amazon category. And it did! Together we accomplished something great.

When the dust settled and the event was done, I sat down to really look at and relish my amazing new book. But, instead of feeling a sense of accomplishment and pride for a job well done, I discovered it was terrible! Not the teaching points within, but the grammar, spelling, and other technical aspects were awful! In my haste to finish on time, and my inexperience in the publishing world, I had not realized how immensely important it is to have a fantastic editor.

Ugh! What had I done?

Yes, there are times when I truly believe that it is better to finish perfectly than to be perfectly finished. But I'd built a publishing division of DPWN. How could this book properly represent that effort unless it was excellent? So, I quickly sent the manuscript to another editor to be reviewed and re-published. Phew! That was close…

I could rest. My book was perfect!

Now, years later, as I review the second version of that book, I can still see many mistakes. Out comes the red pen once again! My goal is to transform this book into one of the best in the networking space.

Two

The second reason I felt compelled to republish this book is that I've gained a new appreciation for the power of stories. Over the years I've learned how valuable stories are, in so many ways, but most importantly when teaching. The greatest storyteller of all was Jesus; He was a master at inspiring and instilling wisdom in His followers through parables.

So, this book will contain new stories sprinkled throughout its pages, from myself as well as from women who have adopted some of its teachings.

Three

Finally, when I was a new networker, I wished I'd learned how to network in school. It would have been truly fantastic if I could have expedited my results and increase my commission checks sooner. Heck, I can remember vividly how scared and lost I felt as a newly single parent, trying to make it on my own without alimony or child support, when my bills totaled more than my income every month. (Yes, things were very different back then, and my lawyer stunk—but that is a story for a different book.) But somehow, things worked out—as they always seem to do.

In hindsight, I see how that situation needed to happen. It is what spurred me on to create what I believe is the best resource for women who need to generate new clients: The Dynamic Professional Women's Network, Inc. It is an organization that combines the best-of-the-best from other organizations into a hybrid community that was originally desinged for working moms who want to build strong business, yet still keep their family a top priority. Of course many of our members are not working moms. I, myself have kids who are adults now, but I believe we've accomplished our goal with flying colors. We are truly one of the best networking resources for women out there.

And so, after 13 years in the industry, I've accumulated a treasure trove of wisdom and experiences that I want to share. I want this book to provide transformational results for my new and future DPWN Members, as well as anyone else who wants to learn how to network. I want them to know, without a shadow of a doubt, what they should do when networking—and more importantly, what they should not do. I don't want anyone to waste their time on efforts that will get them a minimal ROI (return on investment). I want everyone to get accelerated results so that they can start getting new clients right away.

If you would like to learn more about how you can get plugged into our amazing community, visit www.OurDPWN.com.

INTRODUCTION
The Proof
is in the Pudding

Years ago, I would have laughed if anyone suggested that I was going to write a book someday. Communication is not one of my top strengths. Heck, communication—and writing in particular—does not even make it to the bottom of my "strength" list! And yet, I was honored to be invited by Michelle Prince to share my story in the "Dare to Be a Difference Maker" project, back in 2012.

Many people desire to share their story with people who make them feel comfortable: friends, family, possibly even co-workers... People they like and with whom they feel safe. But to share the intimate details of our life with strangers, in a book that anyone can read, is downright scary.

Although my introverted tendencies immediately prompted me to say "No" with a capital "N" and a capital "O", I quickly realized how beneficial having a published book would be for my business. And it was!

Plus, that experience guided me to create a similar project for the women in my network, entitled Overcoming Mediocrity. In this book series, women from many walks of life have the opportunity to share their stories as well. (That, too, is a story for a different book. You can meet these women and learn more about the project at www.OvercomingMediocrity.org)

Once the "Published Author" door was opened to me, my mind was expanded to accept the challenge of writing my own book. I wanted to share the lessons I've learned throughout the years from people who've been a great example for me on what to do… And I also wanted to share what NOT to do. I learned how to network differently than most, and I knew how valuable my insights would be to others.

You see, I learned how to build a networking tribe. Not only was the tribe model more conducive to success for my introverted personality, it also provided me impressive results in the most efficient manner possible. Although I needed to build a business that would provide me with a nice cash flow, the bigger motivator for me was to be able to spend less time networking and building my business, so that I would have more time to spend with my kids and to take care of my home.

What is Your Biggest Networking Challenge?

Many people seem to assume that after they attend a few networking events, collect a few more business cards, and simply add a list of names to their email database, new customers will magically appear. Ta-da!

We all have, at some time in our networking adventures, gathered enough business cards to start a small bonfire. Although this may yield enough heat to roast a small mountain of marshmallows, they probably won't result in much new business. Some of us even get connected with referral groups that are designed to build strong relationships and generate accelerated business opportunities, only to be disappointed with those results as well. We then divert the blame for our failed results conveniently away from ourselves and toward other people, or the group itself. We fail to realize that our results are directly reflective of the efforts we made in the group.

When I started networking many years ago, I was very successful at making these networking blunders, and many others. But over time, I weeded through the plethora of tips learned from other networkers—including the women in my organization—and put together what I have found to be proven strategies that actually work.

Maybe you are brand new to the business networking world, and until recently thought that networks were for connecting computer systems. Or maybe you've surpassed the "newbie" status to become a seasoned professional networker. Either way, the principles I will be sharing in this book will help you.

But… Here it comes… THE BIG BUT!

"But"… no matter how brilliantly I share my networking strategies, resources, tools and principles, they will still remain only strategies, resources, tools and principles—meaning none of them will work—without intentional and consistent practice.

Let's get started.

What I Learned That Can Help You

- First, I needed to become crystal clear about my business goals, and create a personal brand that my clients could connect with.

- I had to understand the specific needs of my ideal client avatar, and I had to accept the fact that I should not be trying to help everyone.

- I needed to find, or build, a quality network of selected partners that I could support and be supported by.

- I had to take ownership of my network and ensure that together we focused on:

  - Building strong relationships with each other.

  - Continually developing a stronger and more expansive network.

  - Properly training each other to buy not only from each other, but to become an extended sales force.

- I had to develop and stick to a networking plan that would ensure that my networking efforts would remain intentional and results-driven. It also had to include a simple system to track my progress.

- I needed to have systems in place to help me leverage my time and make my follow-up more systematic and automated.

Once I grasped all of these principles, I discovered that being a part of a powerful tribe of smart business women brought me far more treasures than I could have ever created alone. And the bonus win was that these same women would become treasured friends that I would cherish forever.

Finding a Tribe is Just the Beginning

In this book I want to share with you the networking expertise I gained during the many-year journey of building my tribe. I grew from a networking newbie to the founder and manager of a successful networking organization.

- I will share with you my tribe networking "secrets," so you too can have the same results with your business networking efforts.

- I will share some basic dos and don'ts, as well as very detailed support for you to join or create your own thriving networking tribe.

- I will provide you with action steps, and quite possibly challenge you with homework, if you are willing to accept that challenge.

I truly believe that I've figured out how to create the perfect marriage of networking and tribe building. I will walk you through the process of creating your own best practices to cultivate your own professional business building culture.

These skills were developed over time. The lessons learned were usually accompanied by discomfort, embarrassment, frustration and fear (like the time I froze and almost fainted in front of an audience of high school girls).

Other lessons were learned in moments of desperation, as I became a single mother, responsible not only for myself, but for two small children. Over time, building this dynamic network of professional women has taught me valuable lessons about leadership, ego and purpose. I will share more about those learning moments in the pages of this book.

I welcome you on this journey. I challenge you to recognize that the only way for you to get the results you desire is to become completely engaged with my system. Don't pick and choose what you want to follow and then expect it to work. You have to follow the process, interact with the appropriate action plans, and check off the steps as you complete them and fill in the blanks as requested.

Congratulations to you for choosing this book! It will guide you in learning about the value of a tribe, and how to find, join and thrive through tribe networking. In doing so, I believe you will find that your tribe will challenge and encourage you to learn, grow and thrive. It's up to you.

CHAPTER 1
The 5 Key Principles of Your 5-Star Network

I love to laugh!

I love funny jokes, funny movies, funny quotes, and laughing together with my friends until our sides hurts. Even though I love laughing myself, I get the most joy out of doing things to make my grandchildren laugh.

Laughter is food for the soul.

One of my favorite actors of all time is Robin Williams.

He was a comedic genius.

I can vividly remember laughing continually to *Mrs. Doubtfire*, *The Birdcage* and *Patch Adams*. And do you remember *Mork & Mindy?* (Nanoo-Nanoo!) That guy was so funny!!

And yet, as we now know, his brilliant life was actually clouded by depression. Robin Williams battled life-long loneliness.

Loneliness is everywhere in our society, and our culture is slowly turning into a relational desert. It's ironic, really, because we must be the most digitally-connected generation of all time. Yet, recently at my church the pastor shared results from a study where nearly half of the respondents said that they experience regular and chronic loneliness.

Half of them!

They responded with comments such as:

- "Nobody knows me well".

- "I feel like I'm surrounded by people, but nobody's actually with me".

- "I feel like I don't have anybody to share life's highs and lows with".

Although we might be hyper-connected digitally, and having social media at our fingertips gives us the ability to connect with thousands of people at any given time, what we're finding is that this digital connection doesn't actually help us with loneliness.

It's just empty calories.

It's like eating ice cream. It tastes really good while we're eating it, but it gives us brain freeze, a stomach ache, or maybe even a sugar headache. And, if you don't live on a treadmill, regular consumption of ice cream will give you an "I can't fit into my jeans anymore" ache.

We may be getting more connected digitally; but relationally we're drifting farther and farther apart.

On another note, according to the most recent statistics from the U.S. Census Bureau, there are more single adults living and working in the United States than ever before in history. In 2017, the U.S. Census[1] reported that there are 110.6 million unmarried people over the age of 18. That's 45.2 percent of the American adult population carrying out their lives to a new set of societal norms; and 53.2% of that group, a staggering 58.8 million of them, are women.

In reality, not only do we have that internal "feeling" of being alone, we actually "are" more alone.

And what about everyone who is not single? How many people of the other 54.8%, who are in a relationship, feel completely alone and isolated? I really think I don't want to know that depressing statistic.

[1] www.census.gov/content/dam/Census/newsroom/facts-for-features/2017/cb17-ff16.pdf

One of my favorite Robin Williams quotes, and the one that sticks with me the most, is, "*I used to think the worst thing in life was to end up all alone. It's not. The worst thing in life is to end up with people that make you feel all alone.*"

I know… It's heavy, right?

On a brighter note.

According to a recent article by Inc. Magazine[2], over the past 20 years the number of women-owned businesses in the U.S. has increased by 114%. That's a staggering 849 new businesses every day!

Great news, right?

Well, it would be… if we, as women, weren't facing a real and challenging dilemma every day.

A disease, really…. And we don't need anyone giving us any freaking statistics about it, do we?

You know how it goes. One moment we're rolling along as the princess of our Disney Kingdom, and then when the need arises, we put on our deflective bracelets and power belt to become an unconquerable warrior taking on the whole world. Every time life gets tough or we want to accomplish something big, we transform into Wonder Woman.

Who else has that insatiable Wonder Woman Syndrome?

Taking care of our families, their health, our health, our homes, being there for our friends, managing conflict like a warrior, and all the while doing it alone because we feel that most people aren't strong enough to hold us up when we waver.

Or we power up and push our own limits to do something bigger than we've ever done before. And we attempt to do that alone as well.

We have this terrible epidemic of loneliness increasing just as steadily as the rise of female entrepreneurship. It is scary!

As women, I believe that we can do ANYTHING that we put our

[2] www.inc.com/business-insider/more-women-entrepreneurs-today-than-20-years-ago-its-troubling.html

minds to. But I believe even more strongly that we can do it better and faster if we unite with other like-minded women. With our treasured tribe of women, who have the same hopes and desires that we do, to build a more successful business.

If you are anything like me, you choose to read a book because of the "promise" it makes in its title or its marketing. And if you are reading this book specifically, you're reading it because you found value in its "promise" to help you build a 5-star network of prospects, clients and brand advocates.

But if you are really like me, you may only read half of the book and then get drawn to a different book, because its "promise" becomes stronger than the former's. Or—if I'm really honest with you—I hop from book to book, because I too easily get just downright distracted.

If this is you as well, I urge you to at least read the first and last chapters before you migrate over to the next bright and shiny book. While chapters two through ten will provide you with valuable principles, resources and systems that will deliver my promise—for you to have a 5-star network of prospects, clients and brand advocates—these chapter will provide you with a strong foundation for them all to build off of.

If you can adopt the following five principles into anything you do, you will most assuredly be more successful; not only in your networking efforts, but in all aspects of your life.

The 5 Key Principles to Having a 5-Star Network are:

- Consistent Time
- Quality Time
- Mutual Trust
- Authenticity
- Systems

Principle #1 > Consistent Time

We all know that consistency matters.

You may decide tomorrow that you are going to get into the best shape of your life, but it won't actually happen if you only commit to vising the gym every day over the next week and then nothing more. Or, if you want to lose 10 pounds, you will need to do more than eat a healthy diet just once in a while.

Anything done without consistency is ineffective.

When I want to create a new and consistent habit, I link it to something I'm already doing consistently.

Over the summer, my grandkids wanted goldfish for the little pond I had by the front door. Well, I think it was more like I wanted the goldfish to make them happy. In the past, I've gotten fish for the little pond, and they usually vanish by the end of the summer season. But this year that didn't happen. Winter was quickly approaching and there were still four healthy fish, happily swimming around in the pond.

GREAT… Now what?

I didn't want the stinkin' fish (who were all now named after my granddaughter's classmates) to become fish popsicles. But the last thing I needed was one more thing to try to remember to do every day. If I forgot to feed the little darlings (I say in jest, of course) they would die anyways. And, if I was going to buy an aquarium, colorful gravel, wiggly water plants and a fish cave, and set them up inside, I would not want them to croak. So, I connected the fish feedings to my dog's breakfast and *voilá!* Now the fish will probably live forever…

IKR!

In our network, we know that consistency is one of the key elements to our success. Our chapter meetings are held two times every month on a consistent schedule. We don't meet every week like other similar networks. We are a women-only group, and as women, we don't need to be in each other's faces every week to make great things happen. We have that dreaded Wonder Woman Syndrome, remember?

Whatever group you are in, make sure it meets consistently on a schedule that's designed to get you results.

Principle #2 > Quality Time

How we focus our time, with whatever we do, will determine the degree of success we will have with it. If we make a commitment to spend every Sunday evening with our family to create more fun and memories, yet we spend the majority of our time together checking Facebook or texting friends, we have the consistency, but not the quality.

Another great example would be: if you plan to meet with a group of people consistently to complete a project, and half of the group either shows up late or leaves early, it would take forever to get the project done. To make matters worse, if the whole time you're together you laugh, tell stories and get very little work done, the project will never be completed.

When you decide to spend your time with a referral group on a consistent schedule, the group has to be intentional, structured and designed for productivity.

Our time is a form of currency, actually. In my mind it is the most valuable currency of all. And every minute we spend on something is actually an "investment" in that effort.

What we put in, we get out.

How are you SPENDING your time?

Are you happy with what you are BUYING with your time?

Principle #3 > Interdependence

Without trust in a relationship, what do we really have? We can lack many things together, but trust is the foundation that the rest of the relationship is built on.

In addition, that trust needs to be mutual. While it should not be our goal to become *dependent* on each other, we need to trust each other so that we become *interdependent* with each other.

I need you, you need me, and we won't let each other down.

That is inter-dependence.

Interdependence leads to stronger and more multi-faceted connections.

Our culture says that independence is a sign of strength. On the contrary, independence does not lead to better connections; it simply pushes others away.

In our network, our goal is to become more than referral partners. We strive to become a 5-star business network that creates life-long friendships.

If you want a 5-star network...

- You need to rely on others and let them rely on you.

- You need to care for others and let them care for you.

- They need to trust you, and you need to trust that they won't let you down.

- We need to lean on each other with matters of high importance.

- We need to hold each other up when we're slipping.

- We need to encourage each other when we're accomplishing something great!

- And, most importantly, we need to hold each other accountable to maintaining our personal values, achieving the highest set of standards, and reaching our own ultimate personal goals.

Contrary to popular belief, I believe that God WILL regularly give us more than we can handle by ourself. That's because we really weren't created to handle everything alone. We've been created to need each other, to bear each other's burdens, and to help each other accomplish our big hopes and dreams together. (And of course to lean heavily on Him.)

I've said this hundreds of times, and I'm sure I'll say it hundreds of times more: "Women can do anything they set their minds to, but they can do it better and faster with the support of other like-minded women."

Principle #4 > Authenticity

One of my most favorite aspects of our community is that our members are extremely loyal to each other, as well as to the organization as a whole. When a non-member attempts to sell us their "stuff" (i.e., products or services) they quickly get shut down. Even though they may have fabulous "stuff", our members know that there will be someone else right around the corner who has the same stuff but is willing to make the commitment. Or, better yet, there is probably a loyal member from a different chapter who has the same stuff.

Our women are authentic with each other. They share their hopes, their dreams, their passions, their beliefs, and so many other aspects of their lives together. They are honest, they are vulnerable, and they invite their team to be included in all dimensions of their life. That is what builds the know, like and trust factor.

So, when a non-member turns on their "marketing switch" in an effort to sell us their stuff, it really isn't about us not wanting their stuff. It's about our ability to "choose" to work with someone we know, like and trust.

Principle #5 > Systems

The final principle to having a 5-star referral network is all about 5-star systems.

An individual's success can be multiplied if there is a system created for others to replicate that result. The following chapters will provide you with our duplicable system, as well as tools, resources and processes for you to have your own 5-star network.

Keep reading… the best is yet to come.

CHAPTER 2
You Don't
Have to Know Them All!

This is, or should be, one of the core values every person should have and cultivate in their life. This principle will be important, not only in our personal lives, but in the business world as well. Like when I found myself as a newly single parent trying to make a living in an over-saturated mortgage industry. And later, when I went on to cultivate a strong community of professional women who strive to create continual streams of connections for each other.

This is what tribe networking is all about.

This is what our DPWN women know.

They don't have to know everything and everyone; they can get where they want just by knowing the right people who know the right people.

They don't have to build their businesses alone. They can align themselves with other strong and successful women.

Their treasured tribe of women will help each other take their businesses to new heights, TOGETHER.

Who Has My Life-Preserver?

"What do you want to do when you grow up, Christie?" This was the question I asked myself over and over again in my teenage years. And yet, I was much older than 18 when I actually had to figure out the answer to that fundamental life question.

Like many others, I went through life after high school checking items off my list that qualified me to claim the title of "Adult." I got my degree, got married, had two adorable kids, built my dream house, and started a family business with my husband. I became really good at adapting my desires to be in alignment with those of my beloved family.

It was only after the circumstances of my life changed, as they eventually do, that I was forced to adapt to those changes and figure out a new direction for my life. More importantly, I needed to find a direction that would allow me to earn a decent income. It was a challenging journey that was filled with questions, uncertainty, fear, doubt and heartache.

Today I learned that:
You never know how strong you are, until being strong is your only choice.
– Bob Marley

At the time, not only was I beginning the journey of my own self-discovery, I was suddenly faced with the reality that I had to do more than just manage my children and home alone; I had to find a job that would allow me to financially support my family. To say I was scared was the understatement of the century. I was literally terrified! I knew I was not the only single parent in the world facing this dilemma, but at the time I felt like I was.

Regardless of how overwhelmed I felt, I knew I would have to rise to the occasion and make something happen. My formal education was in graphic design and marketing. I had also accumulated a good foundation of knowledge, from marketing and managing the internal operations of our family auto repair business with multiple locations. However, based on my resume, I was non-existent. At least I felt as if that were so.

The first leg of my journey brought me to a fabulous Christian company in the mortgage industry that was willing to give me an opportunity. It was a great job filled with wonderful people who had values I could respect and emulate. The only problem with this job was that it was commission-based and it was up to me and my people skills to find and help my customers. The *helping* part was not a problem, but the *finding* part was another story.

I thought of myself as a natural networker. It was second nature for me to share my favorite products or service providers with my family and close friends. But now I had to build a commission-based business by purposefully networking, which was incredibly scary to me. Talking to family and friends is one thing, but since I'm an introvert, having to base my success on purposefully talking to strangers was the last thing I wanted to do.

However, I had no other option but to jump headfirst into the professional business networking world. I attended every networking event I could and joined a bunch of Chambers of Commerce. My calendar got full, so I developed a plan and system for following up with the people I would meet.

I became very proficient at this process. My plan was simple. I would not only schedule my events, but I would also make it a priority to schedule time to follow-up with my new acquaintances, so that I could tell them how great my products and services were. I had a system to make these communications semi-automated and time-efficient. I also developed the perfect plan for what I would do at these networking events, to alleviate the fear associated with talking to these new prospects.

I thought I had it all figured out.

I was very busy, my schedule was full, and I was accumulating a large pile of business cards. It all made me feel like I was being productive.

What Happened Next Changed Everything

You can probably guess what is coming next in this story. You bet! I was busy, but I was not getting the customers I needed to pay my bills and keep my family afloat. Because you are reading this book, I can also predict that you are searching for the same answers that I was: how to get tangible and valuable results with your networking efforts.

I was confusing "busyness" for effective business-building activities.

I became so focused on being proficient at the process of networking that I was failing to track and analyze my results. I was also becoming so busy that I was finding it hard to spend enough time with the customers I did get, because so much of my time was spent in this networking vortex.

Today I learned that:

You cannot manage time, but you can manage how you use the time given to you.

– Author Unknown

Then, one day, I was approached and asked to lead a women's-only referral group. At that time, I was virtually unfamiliar with the concept, but I found the whole idea to be quite ingenious. I wasn't yet ready to step into the leadership role and start recruiting women for this new group. I didn't recognize that the value I would receive from this new venture would justify the time and energy I'd spent to make it happen. But I liked the idea, so I began searching for an existing referral group to join. The only problem was that, because there were so many mortgage specialists in the industry at that time, I was unable to find a group that didn't already have a mortgage specialist. Ugh!

I was so close, yet still so far from finding a solution to build my business. But I was not willing to give up. I really liked the idea of having a team of referral partners who would help me build my business, and allow me to streamline my networking activities. It just wasn't coming together as I had hoped.

After months and months of searching and waiting for a position to open, with no results, I became frustrated. I began to realize that even though it would take more time and energy to lead my own group, it would be worth the investment. Plus, I could have even better results with this plan because I could hand-select my team. I would have complete control to build this new group with quality and dynamic women who were just as focused on growing their businesses as I was.

I was sold!

But, did I really know what I was getting into?

The Super Powers of a Networking Tribe

I was on the right path. I had no idea of the challenges (and ultimately, the incredible results) I was going to get with my new group, but I did sense that I was moving in the right direction. However, it would take years for me to completely recognize how powerful that networking group would become for me in my business and life.

In the beginning, my thoughts were very simplistic. I would get to know these women and they would help me build my business. Like most new networkers, I didn't put much thought into how I would help them build theirs in return. As time went on, my mindset shifted to become more focused on their business, and my feelings for them became so solid that their success just automatically became a high priority for me.

Eventually my team of women became strong supporters of each other. As I realized the power that our group had, I realized I had a new goal: to duplicate our process so that more women could share our experience and results. This was not just a group to me anymore; it was "My Treasured Tribe". I loved these women, and I wanted other women to have their own tribes as well.

While "tribe" has become a buzzword, tribes have really been around since the beginning of time. Only in the last century have we been recognizing that a tribe can refer to so much more than a specific culture, native group or familial clan. Seth Godin published his book Tribes in 2008 (Portfolio Press), reviving the concept that being a member of a tribe can give its members super powers. I know first-hand that it absolutely can.

A tribe is a highly-motivated community that works together to do amazing things. A tribe can be your virtual army of consumers, partners or leaders who have a shared sense of ownership in an outcome that fuels massive, sustained action. A tribe lets you build something that empowers a massive number of people with the purpose to join together to make something extraordinary happen and create new realities.

When you build and leverage a tribe, your business will be more scalable, reach farther, and earn more income exponentially faster and at a fraction of the cost. Tribes do not always have to be focused on building a business. Whatever your focus, when you have a tribe to leverage, you will have an auto-expanding engine of growth and impact.

If every entrepreneur could tap into the power of a tribe to launch or grow their business, the benefits would be game-changing for them.

Keep in mind, a healthy networking tribe should provide you more than just business. Your tribe partners can become role models, advisors, comforters, and provide you with financial assistance, intellectual and social resources, entertainment, accountability, encouragement, celebration, and strength. They can help to streamline your efforts and get you powerful results.

Don't confuse your network with your tribe. That is not to say that your network can't be your tribe and your tribe can't be your network; but it is so much more than that. When you align yourself with like-minded people who mutually support each other, they become your family. In our case, we become DPWN Sisters.

My Lessons Learned

My grandfather was one of the smartest men I've ever known, providing me countless lessons that I have only just begun to recognize. I was only 29 when he left my life, but I have many memories of him that have left lasting impressions on me.

One of the fondest memories I have of him was that he bought a shiny new Mercury Marquis every year. I just thought that was amazing, and far more impressive than the beat-up old Mercury Comet my mom was nursing along. Better yet, he always let me choose whether his next new ride would be white or silver, or whatever color I desired. In hindsight, I realize that he may have guided me a bit to pick the color he really wanted, but at the time I thought the decision was all mine.

As a child, my grandpa was one of the most influential and impressive men in my life. His business required him to wear fancy suits and travel a lot, which I thought was super cool. He was like a Hollywood jet-setter to me, even taking my grandma on frequent vacations to places I'd never even heard of. After every trip, he always brought my brother and me some sort of fun, special souvenir. Even though it was Grandma who lovingly selected every one of those special gifts for us—and also numerous birthday and Christmas gifts—I understood Grandpa to be the financial provider and a person of strength and wisdom.

As a single parent, my mom did the best she could to raise us; but it was my Grandpa who always came to the rescue when the furnace went out, the car needed repairs, or an unexpected bill overwhelmed her tight budget. He was generally not very handy, but he would pick up the phone, make a few calls, and the repair guy would be out in the next few days, or sometimes hours, to fix whatever problem we had. He seemed to always have just the right connections, no matter what the dilemma.

Even though I was impressed by all of the bells and whistles associated with my Grandpa, the strongest impression I have of him was that I believed he was smart about everything, especially money. I would overhear him counseling others on investments and business finances. Back before computers, he helped people with income taxes—calculating their income, expenses, deductions and depreciation on paper, refusing to use a calculator. He counseled my then-husband about a new business idea, and even financed it for us.

One of my favorite childhood memories was the big garage sales held at my grandparents' home every year. They were the biggest and best garage sales in the whole DuPage County area, I thought. We looked forward to these events because it was an opportunity for my brother and I to make a little spending money. We'd clean out our closets and sell our old toys, to make a few bucks that we were allowed to spend however we chose. We didn't have an abundance of toys to sell, but we could always count on Grandpa to save the day with his "mystery gift box" donations.

As a salesman, he drove thousands of miles every month, helping sporting goods stores facilitate mega closeout sales. As an incentive, customers could choose a wrapped "mystery gift box" with a qualified purchase. Every year, he would surprise us with a trunk full of these leftover gifts to sell and receive the profits—Cha-ching!

I mention all of these great things about Grandpa because, as smart as he was, he never even graduated from high school. He grew up in tough times, enduring family tragedies that forced him to be the breadwinner at a very early age.

Can you image that? What would life be like had you been pulled from school in the middle of 5th grade? At the time you may have been happy to be forever finished with spelling, writing and math, but where would you be now if that was the extent of your educational journey?

We all know people who have left a lasting impression on us because of how smart or successful we think they are. People to whom we can reach out for advice when needed. Coaches who can pull the answers out of us, and push us into great places we would never have gone on our own. Mastermind partners who can provide knowledge, resources, insightful answers, moral support, and accountability. Mentors who can provide wisdom, financial guidance and connections that you may have never known even existed. The list goes on and on…

People like my Grandpa may not necessarily be book smart, but they are very wise and extremely street smart. They are also very well-connected and can find the solution to a problem with just a mere phone call. They have learned and lived out the biggest lesson of all: **You don't have to know everything as long as you know the people who do.**

Did you get that?

Today I learned that:
You don't have to know everything as long as you know the people who do.
— Author Unknown

CHAPTER 3
You Don't
Have to Know It All!

I can literally trace every goal accomplished in my life back to a mentor or an individual who helped me achieve it. Entrepreneurs, and especially female entrepreneurs, often think they can—and sometimes that they should—do everything on their own. (We're Wonder Women. Right?) However, not only do we need to partner with others who are in the midst of growing their businesses, we also need to seek out people who have already accomplished the things that we aim to accomplish.

We need to learn from and be mentored by them.

Today I learned that:
There are known knowns. These are things we know that we know. There are known unknowns. That is to say, there are things that we know we don't know. But there are also unknown unknowns. There are things we don't know we don't know.
— Donald Rumsfeld

The guidance we need can come from a variety of sources. Each of them can be extremely effective and transformational in their own right. If you are not willing to settle for a mediocre business, you should become actively engaged in one or more of these different support resources.

What is Coaching and Why Do I Need it?

Simply put, coaching bridges the gap between where someone is now and where they want to be in the future. It's not training, it's not consulting, and it definitely is not therapy. Rather, coaching helps individuals achieve specific goals through a collaborative approach and customized solutions. The work is designed to ensure lasting change and promote continuous growth.

Professional coaching helps people produce extraordinary results in their lives, careers, and/or businesses. Through the process of coaching, a client will deepen their understanding, improve their performance, and enhance the quality of their life.

The coaching relationship is a designed alliance, in which both the coach and the participant are active collaborators and equals in the single pursuit of meeting the client's intended outcomes. When a client finds their own answers, they become more resourceful, more effective, and generally more satisfied. They become more accountable and more responsible, and are far more likely to follow through with actions and apply what they've learned to other scenarios and in other aspects of their life.

I've worked with many different coaches throughout the years. In hindsight, I can see now that the times when my growth stalled was when I was trying to do things on my own. I can even see times when my progress declined due to my inability to recognize some ongoing problems and subsequent solutions. We can't see our own messes accurately, and we just can't seem to find the best and most effective solutions to our own problems. It takes an unbiased, seasoned professional to help us move forward in an expedited and successful manner.

Hiring a coach should be recognized as a necessary business investment, just like hiring an IT Specialist to manage your computer technology needs, or a Graphic Designer to create an effective visual presence for your brand. You should seek out and qualify different coaches for each aspect of support you need throughout the different stages of your business growth journey.

According to the International Coach Federation[3], professional coaching can result in a 70% increase in Improved Work Performance, 61% increase in Improved Business Management, 57% increase in Improved Time Management and a 51% increase in Improved Team Effectiveness. They go on to state that the vast majority of companies (86%) say that they at least made back their investment, and that 99% were "Somewhat" or "Very Satisfied" with their overall experience, and a whopping 96% would repeat the process.

The length of time you should work with a coach should be longer than just a few sessions. It takes at least a few sessions for the dynamics of the relationship to begin forming and for the coach to be able to learn enough about your business to effectively help. Set a goal for a minimum of six months of sessions, and stay committed to following their individual program. Not only should the coach be strategic with their coaching plan, but the client should be prepared with the goals they want to achieve through the partnership, be diligent in tracking the outcomes of each session, and then review the overall progress at the end of the term. At that time, the client may want to continue for another defined term, or find another coach who will be better suited to help them achieve their next level of growth.

A few years ago, I jumped way out of my comfort zone with my newest coach. When I interviewed them, their team and their processes, I quickly became excited about the possibilities for my business. The support they could provide me through their knowledge base, plus the incredible resources that would be at my disposal is what impressed me the most.

[3] http://coachfederation.org/need/landing.cfm?ItemNumber=747

I would finally be able to accomplish my national expansion dreams with their help. I could become a bigger and better resource for the niche of female business owners I wanted to serve.

YES! I was ready to sign on the dotted line. I was... until I saw the price tag positioned just above that dotted line.

To say I had sticker shock would be an understatement. It was not because of a lack of value their program provided. I was actually amazed at the levels of support I would get. I was shocked purely because, up until that point, I had never invested that much in myself, and I didn't think I could afford it.

It was a very scary decision for me!

I am not the type of person who places a high level of worth on money. I know that we all need money to live a comfortable life. More importantly, businesses need working capital to grow and thrive. But in general, I am completely unmotivated by money.

So, I tend to follow my heart when financial decisions need to be made. (The accountants out there are cringing right now.) I don't generally do a thorough due diligence when making major purchases, like I should. (More cringing....)

I don't make rash decisions, but I don't over-analyze the situation and spend hours and hours investigating the pros and cons of every purchase option. I just learn the basics, go with my feelings, do the best to make a smart decision, and then move on. I rarely regret the decision, because this is my M.O. and it works for me. (I make a decision, and then I make that decision right!) But this time I needed to be sure that I was using my head a little more, and not relying on my heart and my desire to make a bigger impact in the world. I needed a plan.

So, I created a simple breakdown of the realistic revenue I could generate in the next six months with this new support. It was like a brand new mini-business plan for a brand-new business model. I tried to create a plan as if it were not for my own business, but for a client. I felt this would help me distance myself from my emotional attachment to the outcome and make a smarter decision.

My new plan exposed a new reality for me. I realized that what I had achieved so far, although not unsuccessful by any means, was not even close to the level of what I felt it could be.

I realize now that I had to get out of my comfort zone to see it. I credit the fear associated with making such a huge investment in my business as the catalyst that brought me to this new place. I could begin to see a new reality, and I knew that if I wanted different results, I needed to go about things in a completely different way.

I knew of Albert Einstein's definition of insanity, and I have always been pretty quick to share this quote with others when I felt they needed to hear it, but it was time for me to heed his brilliant advice. So, I jumped in and made the commitment—not only to invest, but to listen to every teaching, attend every event, complete every assignment and, most importantly, be open to learn.

Today I learned that:

Insanity is doing the same thing over and over again and expecting different results.
— Albert Einstein

At the time, I thought the biggest challenge for me was going to be committing the time needed for the classes and homework. But the learning part really turned out to be the biggest challenge.

The Learning Journey

I love to learn!

I am an avid reader with a pretty expansive book collection, and I enjoy listening to audio books, webinars and podcasts that I find interesting. I also like to attend select business development conferences every year.

A few years ago, I attended an event in Florida because I was ready to take my business to the next level. This event was a little different than any other I have attended. The host had various segments throughout the agenda where she connected with a specific attendee on stage about a challenge they may have been facing. Since I am not, nor have ever been, a hand-raiser, I was shocked when I found myself completely emotional at the microphone, stating my current challenge to this woman in front of her audience of 600 plus.

She asked me a few exploratory questions, some of which were a little uncomfortable. With a nervous and cracking voice, I promptly answered each question with what I thought were brilliant "reasons" why I was doing things a certain way. (My way = the right way.)

After hearing only a few of my responses, or "excuses why," she simply said to me, "Why are you here?"

"Because I want to grow my business," I replied.

"So, you came here to learn how to grow your business?"

"Of course," I said as if it were obvious. I wanted to say "Duh!" but was just too nervous; and I thought it may be a little inappropriate for the circumstances.

Today I learned that:
True humility is staying teachable, regardless of how much you already know.
– Author Unknown

"You have no intentions of growing your business, because you are not here to learn," she then said, calling me out on the table. "I have asked you several questions that should have guided you to see a different perspective, but you instantly replied back to me as if you already know it all. I do hope that I am wrong; but if you don't decide right now that you don't need to always be right, you are going to keep failing. Please prove me wrong. Next." And then she went on to the next person in line at the microphone as if what she had just said was not "earth shattering" to me.

My mind was swirling. *OMG! Who the heck does she think she is? What gives her the right to make that presumption? Wait, was it really a presumption? Could she have been right? Nah! But I have heard similar advice before. Maybe she is right. Maybe I do need to accept being wrong once in a while. Maybe filling my head with content and wisdom from various sources does not make me knowledgeable enough. Maybe part of my learning journey needs to include learning to be wrong so I can re-learn things a different way.*

Truly Wise Mentorship

No matter how smart you are—or how smart you think you are—every entrepreneur needs a good mentor. No matter how unique you think your situation is, somebody, somewhere, has already gone through what you are experiencing right now, and will have invaluable insights that they can share with you. In fact, one of the reasons why some businesses fail and others succeed often comes down to mentoring.

Today I learned that:
A truly Great Mentor is hard to find, difficult to part with, and impossible to forget.
— Author Unknown

A good mentor can have many different roles in your life, and in your efforts to take your business to the next level. The most obvious, yet sometimes overlooked, is to counsel you and provide you with valuable knowledge that you may not have and did not even know that you needed.

"You don't know what you don't know."

Never was a truer sentence ever spoken. When expressing frustration or exasperation, we often find ourselves saying something like, "If I had known that my plane was going to be two hours late, I wouldn't have rushed to the airport," or, "If I had known there was going to be an accident on the freeway, I would have left 30 minutes earlier." Yet, in all these instances, life offers no crystal ball. There's no way of knowing what the future holds, or to be cognizant of something we are unaware of.

It is the same with our businesses. When you have a strong relationship with one or more mentors who can see your business from their perspective, they are able to share valuable wisdom with you, in ways you will not even recognize you need until your eyes are opened in a different way.

Here are a few more ways that good mentors can help you:

- Guide you to find ways to get un-stuck from a problem or place you may not know how to get out of, based on their own past experiences.

- Bring about awareness of a problem from their outsider's view, which will allow you to discover what the problem really is.

- Be a source of inspiration for you, as you recognize their accomplishments as business professionals as well as their contributions to society.

- Allow you to think bigger and have grander visions for yourself, as you spend bits of time in their "bigger" world.

- Have a multitude of connections that will help you in various ways. Ways that you could never even anticipate.

Although most of us can recognize the many benefits of having a mentor or sponsor at our backs to teach, promote and encourage us, we just don't know how to find the right person.

The first thing you need to do is to ask yourself what specific role you want your mentor to provide. It would be helpful to think about, and then write down the answers to, the following questions:

- What problem do you need help overcoming?

- What would you like to learn more about?

- How will the mentorship "look"?

- How often would you like to meet? Where?

- What is the best way to communicate in between meetings?

Be sure that you choose someone who has experience and connections within your industry and is at a level beyond where you are now. You can focus on finding someone who has started a venture that's similar to yours, and who understands the trials and tribulations of building a business like that. Keep in mind that an adviser or consultant who offers their time in return for compensation is not the same thing as a mentor. While paid consultants can be very helpful, true mentors are effective partly because they are only interested in helping others succeed.

Today I learned that:

A lot of people have gone further than they thought they could because someone else thought they could.
– Zig Ziglar

If you don't yet have someone in mind who would be a good mentor for you, make a list of successful people in your field. Is there someone on that list whom you admire and respect? Ask them to lunch or to coffee, or simply ask for 30 minutes of their time for a phone chat.

When you do decide to approach someone, make sure that you don't go in blind. Know what you want to ask and get straight to the point. Explain what excites you about your service or product, be honest about your fears, and ask for feedback.

And don't feel like you have to be limited to only one mentor. While it is not wise to juggle a dozen or more mentors, having two, or possibly even three mentors can allow you to be more specific and effective with each mentor while providing you a vaster array of insights.

Now, once you've gotten the green light from your desired mentor, start thinking about becoming a mentor to someone else who may need your guidance. Even if you feel like you are at the bottom of your hierarchy, or you don't know enough to share, you might find mentees through alumni associations or non-profits where you volunteer. This act of service will also give you a better idea of how to work with your own mentor.

What is a Mastermind Group and Why Do I need That Too?

If you are new to the concept of a mastermind group, then a must-read book is *Think and Grow Rich* by Napoleon Hill (Tarcher, Revised and enlarged, 2005). Hill describes a mastermind group as: "The coordination of knowledge and effort of two or more people, who work toward a definite purpose, in the spirit of harmony." Another more recent book talking about mastermind groups is *Meet and Grow Rich* by Joe Vitale (Wiley, 2006).

Participants bring synergy of energy, commitment and excitement to a mastermind group. The goal is to harness the collective ideas, resources, wisdom and support of a group of like-minded individuals, to which you are held accountable, in order to achieve success faster and more definitively.

What Are the Key Benefits of a Mastermind Group?

- Mutual Support—Groups should be formed around a specific activity; but even with differing goals you'll be able to lean on each other for support. Many times, if your progress slows down on a specific goal, the members of your mastermind group are the only people who really understand what has been going on behind the scenes, and how to give support in spite of your failed efforts.

- Differing Perspectives—Hearing different views from fellow mastermind participants will allow you to see issues you otherwise wouldn't have. Whether you agree with their assessment or not, listening will give you a better understanding of how to improve your approach.

- Resources—Everyone in your group will have access to a different skillset and network of people. Quite often, if you ask for help in your mastermind group, these resources will help you make progress in ways you never could have by yourself.

- Accountability—Your fellow group members will hold you accountable to your goals. In addition, just knowing that you have a regularly scheduled meeting will drive you to make progress. You don't want to be the only person reporting back that you haven't made an effort to move forward.

Additional Benefits of a Mastermind Group:

- Increase your own experience and confidence
- Sharpen your business and personal skills
- Create real progress in your business and your life
- Gain an instant and valuable support network
- Get honest feedback, advice and brainstorming
- Borrow on the experience and skills of the other members
- Receive critical insights into yourself
- Draw on optimistic peer support in maintaining a positive mental attitude
- Be inspired by a sense of shared endeavor—there are others out there!

I have been a part of many mastermind groups, both as a member and as a facilitator. The groups I facilitate offer a combination of masterminding, peer brainstorming, education, accountability and support in a group setting to sharpen your business and personal skills. By bringing fresh ideas and different perspectives, masterminds can help you achieve greater levels of success.

CHAPTER 4
Introverts Connect – Extroverts Collect

Let's learn a little bit about both Introverts and Extroverts so we can be more successful interacting and connecting with each other in our tribes. Since I've created a few strategies that I use to adapt when networking, I would like to share them with you.

When I was younger, I enjoyed playing in solitude. I would sit and play for hours, dressing and re-dressing my Barbie dolls with their prettiest outfits. I would make sure their wardrobe and hair styles would pass even the toughest critiques from the most expert judges, as they strutted up and down their makeshift New York fashion show runway. And then in my teenage years, I enjoyed drawing and painting. I would spend endless hours alone exploring my creative side and mastering the techniques needed to produce beautiful art that I would give as gifts to my family and friends. I also enjoy reading. There is nothing more enjoyable for me than to curl up with a good book and escape into the storyline.

You see, as an introvert, I am more naturally drawn towards activities that do not involve others. It is the solitude that energizes me.

I always believed that I was inferior to others because I was not drawn toward making friends and playing with them. I felt odd because I preferred being alone. When I did wind up in situations where I'd have to interact with people I didn't know well, it was always awkward. My underdeveloped social skills would often result in uncomfortable moments if the focus was directed towards me. I preferred listening, watching, and learning about others, instead of them learning about me. I thought I was BORING!

Being an introvert was not a personal choice for me. I was born this way, and it's not a flaw in my character. I cannot will myself or work harder to be the life of a party, to be a social butterfly, or even to be comfortable sharing about myself with strangers. I will probably always feel a bit challenged when making small talk with people when I first meet them. But, because I learned from the book, *The Introvert Advantage* (Workman Publishing Company, 2002), that I am like this is due to my genetic disposition, I can stop feeling disappointed in myself and can focus on how to compensate in other ways. I also know that the few friends I do have are close friends and I am extremely loyal and committed to those relationships.

Here are a few classic characteristics of introverts like myself, along with a few of the extroverts of the world.

Classic Characteristics of Introverts

- Often feel drained when having to interact with a large group of people or with people they may not know.

- Focuses inward to gain energy and recharge their battery.

- Draw energy from their internal world of ideas, emotions and impressions.

- Often immerse themselves in their tasks. Are reflective, focused and self-reliant.

- Calculate how much energy something will take, decide how much they need to conserve, and plan accordingly.

- Prefer clearly-defined roles.

- Over-prepare by accruing as much information as possible in an attempt to avoid blank moments.

- Have fewer and more intimate relationships.

- Prefer one-on-one discussions or leading a group discussion over participating as part of a larger group or roaming in a crowd.

- Are calm and self-contained.

- They enjoy listening and they tend to think before they speak.

- Like to know details about what they are experiencing.

- Are capable of being skilled public speakers or actors/actresses.

Classic Characteristics of an Extrovert

- Gain energy from large groups of people, regardless of if they know anyone or not.

- Thrive on a variety of stimuli.

- Cast a wide net when accruing knowledge, experience and relationships.

- Tend to multi-task rather than immersing themselves in one task.

- Like to know a little bit about everything.

- Are outwardly-directed. They tend to be more comfortable thinking and talking at the same time.

- Prefer group discussions.

- Focus more on people and events, especially if the events will have lots of people.

- Value sharing with others even with new acquaintances.

- Need diversions to keep them engaged.

- Find public speaking easy.

Knowledge is Power

Remember Claire from the beginning of this book? I think it's safe to say that she was definitely an introvert. I'm sure she was so nervous the first day she visited our group because we were all strangers to her .

In fact, that is one of the reasons why introverts typically find referral exchange groups so appealing. They love the fact that they don't have to step out of their comfort zone by attending big networking events with a bunch of people they don't already know. They are able to build relationships with people over time, so that they become trusted business partners and loyal friends. And when a referral is received, they are able to reach out to that potential new client with complete confidence, because they know that their call is expected. The fear is reduced, if not removed altogether.

Now that you have been equipped with some basic knowledge about these two personality types, you will be able to customize your own networking efforts accordingly.

Being an introvert has given me firsthand experience on how I can be the most successful with my networking efforts.

For the introverts of the world, I want to share these tips with you.

My Introvert Action Plan

1. Face the Fear—Be confident that, with the right skills, you can become comfortable networking.

2. Strategically Scheduled Networking—Take a quick inventory of the different types of networking functions available to you. Although it is important for you to choose opportunities that will provide you with optimal results, you will also want to consider schedules, making sure they fit with your introverted style. Since you recognize that you will be feeling drained after a highly interactive event, you will want to target evening events, if possible. If there are great events

that happen during the morning or lunch hour, try to create a light schedule following the event. If that is not possible, plan to take at least a 30-minute break to meditate, pray, or just enjoy doing nothing afterward, so you can add a little juice back to your energy level.

3. Prepare Well—Make sure you are fully prepared to attend every event. Make it a point to plan your attire in advance, wear a pre-prepared name tag, have a full supply of business cards, pre-register, clarify your goals, and do something to help you feel grounded before the event. It only takes one thing being out of place in your mind to throw off your rhythm and make it harder for you to connect naturally with others.

4. Go with Someone—It's always best to attend networking events with a buddy, regardless if you are an introvert or an extrovert. However, introverts will feel even more comfortable and have better results if they have the security of attending networking events with someone they already know.

   Be aware: if you chose the buddy option, I challenge you to not sit or hang out together the whole time. The best strategy is to work the room together by splitting up and making strategic introductions for each other when appropriate.

5. Be Approachable—Do not put unnecessary stress on yourself by thinking that you'll need to be the interaction initiator. Instead, just focus on having good eye contact and smiling at everyone you pass by. You will be surprised at how many of them will initiate a conversation with you. Good eye contact conveys confidence and interest in others. Adopting this exercise will also help you develop discipline at remaining focused when conversing with someone.

6. Approach Someone Alone—Even though it may be scary to be the interaction initiator, it will be much easier to approach someone

who is standing all by themselves. They are probably just as scared as you... or quite possibly, even more so. This is always a helpful strategy for me, because it takes me out of my scared mindset and puts me in the mindset of a helper.

7. Take a Recharge Break—I almost always find an opportunity to slip away and take a mini-recharge break. Even if it may only be to the restroom, taking that little rest from networking will provide you with the energy to return with a new and fresh perspective.

8. Be Equipped to Engage—Just like you need to be fully prepared with the networking tools listed in item #3, you need to be just as equipped with ways to engage and remain engaged with others during the events. Try these tips:

   - When in a food line, hand a plate to the person behind you.

   - Before getting a drink or snack, ask whether anyone nearby would like something also.

   - Compliment someone's unique item, such as eyeglasses, tie, jewelry, etc.

   - Compliment special qualities, such as a bright smile or positive energy.

   - Ask about accomplishments.

   - Make a point of introducing people who you think would connect.

   - Share other networking events.

   - Offer to provide follow-up information on a discussed topic.

Here are some tips for the extroverts of the world. You may think: *As an introvert, how could I possibly offer advice to all of the social butterflies out there?* Well, given the fact that introverts are naturally observers, I can tell you that it would be wise to take heed of my advice.

Plus, introverts tend to be attracted to extroverts. I know people who are very comfortable with the social aspect of networking, but they miss the ball on many levels and don't get many clients out of their efforts. These tips are meant to help them get better results.

Extrovert Action Plan

1. Face the Reality—You are someone who can connect easily with others, and you enjoy knowing that your business Rolodex is pretty extensive. You may however, be surprised to find out how shallow those connections really are. This can be an unsettling thought to most extroverts. With a little redirected effort, though, those contacts can become a gold mine for you as you rebuild your referral network.

2. Strategically Schedule Your Networking—Although you may want to attend every event and meet as many new people as possible, be sure to only schedule networking events when you are able to also schedule time in your calendar for follow-up.

3. Stay Focused on Purpose—Since you tend to thrive on stimuli, it may be hard for you to remain engaged with someone when you are talking to them about their business. Keep a standard list of 3–5 questions you need answers to before you move on to the next person. Your questions will help to keep you engaged during each exploration session and focused on the person you are meeting.

4. Create Small Yet Deep Goals—Arrive at each new networking opportunity with a purposeful plan to meet a select few new contacts, and learn as much about them as possible.

5. Under-Commit and Over-Deliver—Don't make the mistake of making promises to everyone you meet when networking. Doing this will only saddle you with the reputation of being untrustworthy

and unprofessional. You will undoubtedly wish to fulfill all of the commitments you make to support others; but the reality is, you will either forget or get too busy to deliver as promised. This does not mean you have an excuse to not even try to make promises; it means that you should try even harder to deliver, without an unmanageable amount of upfront expectation.

6. Follow-Up is a Must—Extroverts tend to have very engaging and magnetic personalities. People like to be liked by extroverts because they are bubbly and dynamic. The flaw is that the higher you pump someone up, the harder they fall when you let them down—so DON'T! Since you are now under-committing and remaining focused on building deeper relationships with others, your follow-up efforts are the most crucial part of all of your networking efforts.

Each member of your tribe is either an introvert, an extrovert, or a combination of both. It's not important to figure out what each person is; it's important to understand that people look at things and react to things in different ways, based on their personalities. It is the balance of introverts and extroverts working off each other's strengths that makes a tribe successful.

CHAPTER 5
The Basic Mechanics
of Networking

In order to better understand the workings and power of a networking tribe, we should first dissect some of the dos and don'ts of basic networking.

When people hear the word *networking,* they tend to come up with a vast array of meanings based on their current circumstances and personal histories. If you were to ask an unemployed college grad, they would most likely recognize networking as the best way to make the connections that will help them land the job of their dreams. If you ask a stay-at-home mom who has just moved to a new city, she will most likely be implementing her networking skills to find a new physician for her family or to find the best playgroups for her kids. Corporate executives will network to better position themselves for higher paying and more influential jobs, while business professionals network to cultivate additional business opportunities.

Although networking is practiced by many people for many reasons, most people have never been exposed to formal business networking. Those who have, most likely have never had any formal training to ensure that their efforts are not made in vain. I meet many people who tell me how frustrated they are that they are just not getting the results they want from their networking efforts.

With any new activity we strive to master, it's important to have a strong and solid foundation. Networking is no exception. By establishing your reasons why and your desired results, your networking efforts will be maximized. It's really important to know what you want to accomplish through networking before you even start. Desired results can be anything from an introduction, a partnership, or a joint venture opportunity.

Let's look at what I feel is the best definition of business networking.

> *Business Networking: A socioeconomic, learned skill by which like-minded business professionals build relationships with each other to recognize, create, or act upon business opportunities together.*

And now, let's take some time to dive a bit deeper and break down each part of this definition.

*"A **socioeconomic**, learned skill by which like-minded business professionals build relationships with each other to recognize, create, or act upon business opportunities together."*

1. While networking is a very social activity, we need to remain focused on the purpose: economic outcome. Let's face it: regardless of the type of business we have, we are looking to grow it through networking in order to generate more business and increase our profits. However, because we don't usually have a system to measure the direct profits that are obtained as the result of our networking efforts, we sometimes lose our focus. We get caught up in the social aspect of networking and not the economic value.

*"A socioeconomic, **learned skill** by which like-minded business professionals build relationships with each other to recognize, create, or act upon business opportunities together."*

2. Yes, networking is definitely a learned skill. It is one of the most powerful skills that we can develop to expand our businesses; and yet, it is a skill that is not taught in any kind of formal educational platform, including trade schools, colleges, and universities. This lack of education is the reason so many professionals spend more time on networking than they should.

*"A socioeconomic, learned skill by which **like-minded business professionals** build relationships with each other to recognize, create, or act upon business opportunities together."*

3. If you approach building your referral network the same way that you would approach hiring and adding business partners for your business, you will assemble an amazing team of referral partners. You are a rock-star in your profession, and you do not need to spend time dabbling in relationships with just anyone. You must set goals and remain focused on assembling your own personal Rock-Star Referral Team.

*"A socioeconomic, learned skill by which like-minded business professionals **build relationships** with each other to recognize, create, or act upon business opportunities together."*

4. In order to have a strong referral network, you must not only do business with your referral partners, but also develop strong relationships with them until you become invested in their personal success. You must get to know about them, their families, their interests and their businesses, so that their success becomes almost as important to you as your own.

*"A socioeconomic, learned skill by which like-minded business professionals build relationships with each other to **recognize, create, or act upon business opportunities together."***

5. This is where most networking partnerships fail. It is the step that will take the most time and demand the most dedication from you. This is the step that, if applied, will lead you down the road to success much further and more quickly than you ever imagined. You will need to meet regularly with your Rock-Star Referral Partners to strategize ways to formally support, encourage and market each other.

What is Business Networking NOT?

Now that we have taken the time to analyze my definition of business networking, it is important to pause for a moment to review a list of what networking is not.

Networking is Not a Time to:

1. Sell Yourself or Promote Your Products or Service

Very, very rarely will you cross paths with someone who is ready to do business with you when you meet them at a networking event. Most people are mainly there to promote themselves and make connections. Your self-promotion will either fall on deaf ears or will be received poorly by true networkers.

2. Focus on Eating and/or Drinking

While there will most often be food and beverages at your networking events, consume them casually, being careful not to overindulge or to spill them on yourself. You should always practice proper eating etiquette.

3. Find a Date

While this may seem obvious to some, and possibly even silly to mention, I have seen or been approached by far too many people with this exact purpose in mind. Make sure you are always dressed in appropriate professional business attire and not your night club wardrobe. When chatting with networkers of the opposite sex, be sure to avoid being overly flirtatious, regardless of your current relationship status.

4. Aggressively Distribute your Business Cards

Don't hand out your cards as if it were a contest or as if they are a valuable commodity. Only ask for others' cards when you are conversing with them, and offer yours only when asked.

5. Talk More About Yourself Than the Other Person

Attempt to be the one asking all of the questions when you have connected with someone new. You should have a list of standard questions to ask if you are not an easy conversationalist.

6. Complain About and/or Criticize Anything or Anyone

Never utter even one word of negativity to a new networking friend. They don't care about the heavy traffic or how mean your boss is. They will see you as a Negative Nellie, regardless of whether your complaints are valid or not. You also don't know who they know; you could be speaking ill of a friend or colleague.

7. Share Too Much and Bore People with the Minor Details of Your Business

Your new acquaintances only want an overview of what you do and your USP (Unique Selling Proposition). It is important to never use industry jargon, even if you assume they know it.

8. Monopolize Someone's Time and Not Allow Them to Connect with Others

Some people may be too shy or polite to dismiss themselves from a long conversation with you, even though they may want to. Give yourself a five-minute limit with each person you meet and then move on to meet someone new.

9. Promise Things You Can't or Don't Deliver

It is much better to under-promise and over-deliver than to make even one promise you don't follow up on. You will be seen as unreliable and not a good referral partner.

10. Interrupt Others While They are Talking to Introduce Yourself

If you want to meet someone who is already engaged in a conversation, or break into a group that is deep in conversation, it is best to observe quietly and to become involved at an appropriate time. Do not interrupt boldly as if you are more important than them and their conversation.

11. Hang with Your Friends or People that You Already Know

It is great to attend networking events with a friend, but never sit at the same table together. Instead, focus your efforts on introducing the people you meet to your friend. Always split up and work the room separately. This allows you both to maximize your connections and to be seen as a true connector.

12. Expect the People You Meet to Help You When You Have Not Helped Them

You have to be a true Go-Giver before most people will even want to help you.

13. Grow Your Mailing List

Never-ever-ever add people to your e-mail list without asking their permission to do so. Just because they gave you their card, that does not mean that they gave you permission to mass email them. That is SPAM!

It is said that we all have a contact base of 250+ people to whom we can reach out when a certain need arises. That would be your initial network. These are your friends, family, co-workers, church associates, and the people you've gotten to know from the local Chamber of Commerce or local networking events. You also can build your network with people you meet at your kid's sports activity, at school, or even with someone you meet while sitting at your doctor's office. If you are an extrovert, I'm sure you have many stories about how you met someone who turned out to have a great company you could do business with. Maybe you were able to direct them to one of your trusted referral resources.

A networking tribe, however, is so much more than a business network. That is why they can be so productive and are extremely desirable. This tribe, in essence, is that inner circle of your network that will make the real transformation in your business.

Define Your Networking "White Hot Why."

At this point, you may feel as I did so many years ago. You are networking your tail off, but getting poor results in relation to the time and energy you are spending. You feel like your networking is not really working. You're busy, but your just not getting enough business.

Many business people jump headfirst into the networking game. They join a Chamber of Commerce and/or other professional networking organization, register for an event or two, order a stack of business cards, and think they are set. They attend random events, pass out numerous business cards, and delude themselves into thinking that their ideal clients will start knocking down their doors. They're missing one very important key point to achieve their networking goals. They do not have a big enough *Why*.

Who is Samuel Pierpont Langley?

He was an American astronomer, physicist, the inventor of the bolometer, and a pioneer of aviation. In the early 1900's Pierpont was slated to be the first man to pilot an airplane. He was a senior officer at the

Smithsonian Institution and a Harvard mathematics professor. Some of the most powerful men in business, including Andrew Carnegie and Alexander Graham Bell, were among his friends. He was given a $50,000 grant from the war department and $20,000 from the Smithsonian to fund his project, the equivalent of nearly $2 million today. His success seemed inevitable.

However, only a few hundred miles away, Wilbur and Orville Wright were working on their own flying machine. Their passion to fly was so intense that it inspired the enthusiasm and commitment of a team of humble yet dedicated men to rally together to help make their vision a reality. And it worked!

How did the Wright brothers succeed and fly on December 17, 1903, when the better-equipped, better-funded and better-educated Langley team could not? It was not luck; it was not skill; it was because they were successful at inspiring their team to share their vision. They had a *Why*, and their *Why* was contagious.

My *Why* at the beginning of this journey was to create a structure that would cultivate synergistic relationships with other professional women, to grow my business and support my family. I was a newly single parent facing the challenge of supporting my two kids alone. My *why* was huge! But then, after time, it shifted from me and my family's needs to include the additional needs and whys of my members. This is also similar to the whys of the Chapter Directors that lead the women in their DPWN chapters. While building their businesses is why they joined DPWN as members, inspiring and supporting others is why they became leaders.

In the book *The Compound Effect* (Vanguard Press, 2012), Darren Hardy uses the following example to vividly display why having a powerful *Why* is so important in motivating us to do things we may not have otherwise done. In this book, Darren asks us: If he were to lay a 10-foot wide wooden plank down on the ground, would we walk across it for a $20 reward? Sure, we would. Because that is an easy task to earn a quick reward. There really is no risk.

But if he were to lay that same plank between two high-rise buildings, would we still be willing to walk across that small and possibly unstable wooden plank for a $20 reward? No way! We wouldn't, even consider the notion because the risk is far greater than the reward.

He then proceeds to ask us: If we were on top of one of those buildings, and our child was stranded on the other side, crying in terror as that building was being engulfed by flames, would we then be willing to cross that same bridge? Of course, we would! And at record speed, without much thought to the small size or stability of that plank. The safety of our child becomes our enormous "WHY" and overshadows any potential risk.

Why is Your Networking Not Working?

While I've given you some important tips for improving the results of your networking efforts, I've yet to share the pivotal key of truly successful tribe networking. Think of those busy, yet unskilled, networkers passing out business cards in a frenzy. They are so focused on their own wants and needs that they forget this golden rule of networking. If you don't really let this tip sink in, you will be struggling just like them.

Today I learned that:

All things being equal, people will do business with, and refer business to, those people they know, like and trust.

— Bob Burg

What is the Golden Rule of Networking?

During the first few years of our DPWN journey, I was extremely fortunate to meet Bob Burg, whom I believe is the top expert on relationship networking. One of my friends saw him speak at a conference and was impacted so greatly by what he learned that he asked Bob to speak to my group. Bob was receptive to the idea, and when I contacted him, we worked out the details for me to become a city partner for him in the Chicagoland area. During our numerous phone calls, I instantly felt a unique closeness to him. It became obvious to me that he actually cared about helping me and supporting the women of our membership organization. He genuinely wanted to add value to them and teach them about the Golden Rule of Networking.

That introduction was the beginning of one of the most valuable relationships I've made so far in my professional journey. Not only does Bob have a head full of wisdom that he has shared with us throughout the years—through his *Endless Referrals* and Go-Giver series of books (Portfolio publishers)—but he's been an invaluable mentor and connector for me. He is truly a living example of the philosophies he teaches.

That very first year he presented to our group, he arrived at the event early to greet and mingle with the attendees before it started. He spent time with as many people as he could. If you've ever had to speak to a group, you were probably so focused on your presentation that you never even considered meeting and learning about other people before your talk. But, Bob enjoys learning about and helping others. Mingling with the guests had become a natural routine for him, and it impressed the heck out of those who were able to spend time with him that day!

Even more impressive, was the way he started his presentation. He began by asking the audience to stand if he had had the privilege of speaking with them during that initial open networking time. He then went around the room and asked them to sit down as he recalled not only their first, but their last names as well. The initial group standing consisted of about 40 men and women. At the end of this exercise, he had recalled every name but just a few—which he was even able to remember with small hints. I don't know about you, but I have a hard time remembering what I ate for dinner yesterday, let alone remembering the first and last names of people I met while I was mentally preparing to speak to a group of over 200 business professionals! But he did it with flying colors.

Bob's presentation that day was not about creating memory skills to be able to remember the names of people we meet. That was just how he opened his Endless Referral System talk, so the audience recognized the value of relationship networking. He spoke about creating a group of "Personal Walking Ambassadors" who truly desire to help you achieve expediential growth in your business.

He shared multiple reasons why building a strong referral business is the best way to grow your business. It is easier to set appointments and close deals with referred prospects than other prospects. Referred prospects are less worried about price and more concerned with value. Unlike other prospects, referred prospects are much more likely to be long-term loyal customers. And most importantly, referred prospects are more likely to give you additional referrals from their contact sphere, because that is how they met you.

When you focus your efforts on gaining customers through referrals as opposed to other marketing avenues, you will most likely have the highest quality customer base. Furthermore, it will continue to multiply each year, while your referral generating efforts can decrease. This is simply because eventually the majority of your new customer acquisitions will be the result of pure organic growth received by referrals from your current customer base.

How to Find Your Quality Network

There are many opportunities out there for business professionals to meet and network with each other. With so many options, it's so easy to become overwhelmed, or—even worse—to get involved with too many groups, become overcommitted and become effectively ineffective at them all.

A few of these opportunities are:

- Chambers of Commerce
- College/Fraternity Alumni
- Industry Associations
- Philanthropic Foundations
- Religious Affiliations
- Networking Events
- Trade Shows
- Conferences and Workshops
- Internet Topic or Friend Groups
- Friends and Family
- Referral Exchange Organizations

I believe that each of the above options can be effective and extremely rewarding, depending on your specific business. Make it a point to define your ultimate goals before you choose, so that you will select a group that will help you get what you are looking for. Some meetings are based more on learning and/or volunteering rather than on strictly making business connections.

Visit as many groups as possible that spark your interest. Notice the tone and dynamics of the groups. Are the members engaged? Do they seem to be supportive of one another? Are you impressed with the leadership? Do you feel that the leaders are just going through the motions, or are they also engaged with the members and the overall group? Many groups will allow you to visit a time or two before joining.

Once you decide on your best networking option, be sure that you take on and commit to a volunteer position with them for at least the first year. This is the best way to get connected, stay visible and give back to group that benefits you. Once again, do not get overcommitted; that is the quickest way to become labeled as a networking "taker." Although it would let you meet many people, and possibly land a client or two, you would be virtually ineffective at supporting them as you should.

Even if you stopped reading here and applied the principles I've already shared, you most likely would experience a dramatic increase in successful networking. And yet, we are about to kick it up a notch… by realizing the value in building relationships that not only benefit you professionally, but in all aspects of your life.

Relationship Networking – Expedited Results!

My experience is that the strongest and most numerous referrals are generated through referral exchange groups. A referral exchange group is an organization that has several different chapters whose members commit to supporting and generating business for the partnering members of that specific chapter. Each of these chapters or groups meets on a regular schedule, runs independently, is highly structured and tracks its overall productivity. The chapters have a membership base of success-oriented business professionals who do not compete with each other and are complimentary. Together they set goals to develop personally, help each other's businesses grow with valuable referrals, and assist each other by providing counsel in their particular areas of expertise. This is how you are going to build your successful networking tribe.

Although I believe that a referral exchange group is the best way to build a strong referral business, in order to effectively take advantage of this great resource you must focus your efforts in the right direction. You can't just sign on the dotted line, show up at the meetings and expect to get results… you have to do a bit more than that.

If you want to learn more about the structure and policies of our community, visit www.OurDPWN.com.

CHAPTER 6
Clarifying and Defining Your Networking Goals

At the beginning of every year, the topic of resolutions and goal-setting always comes into everyone's minds. Although I am not a proponent of resolutions, I am a firm believer in setting goals, and have seen firsthand how powerful this exercise can be.

Unfortunately, most people are more diligent about making their grocery lists than they are about designing their lives. Even more troubling, those who actually go through the process of defining their goals don't take the next steps to ensure those goals are achieved.

It's just like the letters we mailed off to the North Pole every year when we were children, listing our most desired toys of the season. We entrusted that sacred envelope to our mailman for safe delivery, and presto!—our new toys appeared under the tree on Christmas morning every year. We gave little thought to how that happened during those magical years; we just trusted in the outcome. Unlike our Christmas list, it is imperative that we not only clearly define the goals we want to achieve, but we take the proper action necessary to ensure their fulfillment.

Let's take this goal-setting and achievement process as it applies to our networking activities. We want to ensure that we have a way to quantify our objectives and results so that we can track our progress and spend our efforts wisely.

The first step of this process is to clearly define our business goals, so that we can create a plan for our networking activities that supports those goals. Every year I create a Microsoft Word document that lists my personal and professional goals, devoting one page for each. I've been doing this for many years now, and have found it to be a very helpful technique to remain consistent with this process. Although I'm an "idea person" and I like to continually improve things, this process should remain simple and very precise. It also needs to be a retrievable working document, so you can update your goals over the years and review your progress.

When setting your goals, they should be BIG, EXCITING and WILDLY AMBITIOUS GOALS (What I call my BEWAGs). This is so important, yet so often overlooked in the goal-setting process. It is okay for some of your goals to be common, like getting a new car, going on a vacation, obtaining a promotion or growing your business. But why not reach for the moon with most of your goals? Why not strive for outcomes way bigger than you would have ordinarily desired?

Today I learned that:
If your dreams don't scare you, they aren't big enough.
– Author Unknown

You should literally be embarrassed to share some of your goals with the world. Don't just set a goal to increase the year-end revenue in your business by 20%; strive to double or even triple it. Don't be happy with just getting a new car; slap a photo of a hot red Ferrari on your goal board. If you really don't want a red Ferrari because it is too pretentious, then slap two photos of your dream car on the board and strive to donate the second car to a worthy charity. You would be surprised to see how much more you will accomplish by stretching your brain in this way.

How Can Your RAS Help You Get Real Results?

Here's a quick and very simplistic science lesson that explains how goal setting works in our brains.

Your RAS (Reticular Activating System) filter is a set of nuclei connected in the brain. It plays a very important role in the human body, controlling functions such as breathing, sleeping, waking, and especially the beating of the heart. Another name for the RAS is the Extrathalmic Control Modulatory System. The RAS is hardwired into our brains. Think of it as a default program within our brains that quickly focuses our attention based on the information being presented. It actually acts as a filter between our conscious and subconscious minds.

Every day, we are exposed to billions of forms of sensory input. Our minds would be completely overloaded if we were to be consciously aware of all of those stimuli, so our RAS filter blocks out 99.9% of all unfamiliar data. It takes instructions from the conscious mind and passes them on to the subconscious. For example, the instruction might be, "Listen for anyone saying 'thunderstorm'," or "look for yellow trucks." Likewise, when we are in a crowded room, we are naturally wired to listen for our own name.

Harnessing the Power of Your RAS Can Be an Essential Tool for Achieving Goals

You can deliberately program your RAS by choosing the exact messages to send from your conscious mind. For example, you can say affirmations or visualize your goals. Napoleon Hill said that we can achieve any realistic goal if we keep on thinking of that goal, and stop thinking any negative thoughts about it. He explains that if we keep thinking that we CAN'T achieve a goal, our subconscious will help us NOT achieve it.

Your RAS cannot distinguish between real events and synthetic reality.

It believes whatever message you give it. Imagine that you're going to be giving a speech. If you practice giving that speech and then visualize it being very successful with a standing ovation from the audience, this pretend practice should improve your ability to give an effective speech.

Or, let's say that you are shopping for a car. Your last car was a black sports car. It was a good car for you at the time, because you had plenty of time to care for it and keep it looking shiny and new. But, now you are now thinking that it may be better to buy a white car because you just don't have the time anymore to wash and wax a new black car. You never even noticed white cars before, because your eyes were always drawn to darker cars that resembled your hot black sports car; but now it seems as if every other car on the road is white. And if you are also looking for a hybrid car like a Prius, you;re sure to see every single White Prius that comes near you on the road, even though you never even noticed them before.

Apply BEWAGs to Your Networking

Would you like to have noticeably greater results with your future networking efforts? Of course, you would. But expecting to get them with the same old techniques is just like Einstein's definition of insanity that we read in Chapter Three: "Doing the same thing over and over again and expecting different results." So, let's do things differently together.

Have you ever set BEWAGs for your networking efforts?

The following parameters can be used for networking, for building your business, or for accomplishing any ambitious goals.

- **Are Your Goals Specific?**
  Do you have a specific number of new clients you want to gain, or a specific amount of business you want to transact from your tribe?

- **Are Your Goals Measurable?**
  It is important that you set a time frame for your results. You will

need to spend a majority of time investing in your tribe when you first join, so the time frame for your first year will need to consider this aspect. The amount of time it takes for you to learn and support your tribe partners will vary depending on the size of your tribe.

Whether you join an existing group or start your own group, you should focus mostly on learning about your tribe partners before you expect them to support you. Neglecting this step is the biggest mistake people make when connecting into a networking tribe. We will touch on this in more detail later in this book.

- **Are Your Goals Obtainable?**
Are they big, yet realistic? They should stretch you, yet not be so lofty that you never reach them (that can be completely demotivating).

- **Are Your Goals Much Bigger Than Last Year?**
Increase your goals each year on a curve that keeps progressing and pushes you to achieve more.

- **Are There Goals on Your List That are Too Scary to Think About or That You Are Embarrassed to Share with Your Friends, Family or Colleagues?**
If not, then you need to go back and re-work your goals to include some that will push you out of your comfort zone.

The final two steps in the Goal Achieving Process, unfortunately, are the steps most people fail to implement: to create a specific action plan, and to have a process for accountability.

Creating an action plan is not like creating a list for Santa to deliver. Creating goals for your business means more than wishing for them to come true. What better way to ensure their fruition than to have a specific implementation plan? Failing to do so would be like creating a goal to lose 25 pounds and then not creating a specific plan that would outline your specific weekly exercise program and daily eating plan. It would also be like planning a big trip to California and then getting in your car, driving down your block, and then expecting to arrive at your destination without mapping out the roads you need to take to get there or plugging the address into your GPS.

To achieve your business growth goals, be sure to define your networking plan before you actually begin networking. Most networkers tend to be reactive with these efforts rather than pro-active. They may have a new product they are looking to gain exposure for, or they may need to reach a certain sales quotas. They then sign up for the next chamber luncheon, promoting themselves, expecting miracles to happen. I am sure that is not what you do; it is what they do. Right?

As we discussed earlier, if our overall goal is to attract and keep loyal customers, why would we not be conscientiously creating the best plan possible? Why would we not be reviewing that plan and refining it as needed based on its success or failure rate?

If you include participation in an association related to your industry as a part of your plan, determine how many events you plan to attend in the upcoming year, and how involved you want to get in the leadership of that association. Define how much money and time you want to invest before you actually begin participating, and then stick to that plan. If you decide to focus your energies into a Chamber of Commerce, follow that same process as well; ditto if you realize that a referral group like DPWN is the best plan for you.

Just keep this in mind: your investment must be adequate for your desired results. You can't get in that car for your big California trip with only 50 bucks in your wallet for gas and only 16 hours allotted for the trip. Just like everything in life, you will get out exactly what you put in with your networking efforts.

Make sure your mindset around networking is focused on investing and not just being busy and having fun. Get involved in a deeper level with whatever you decide. Don't just show up. Take ownership of the choices you make, and invest properly to ensure the overall success of those choices.

Finally, you need to make sure you have a process for accountability with your networking efforts. If you work for a company, you will have a supervisor or a boss who will be monitoring your time and financial investment. If you are self-employed this is a step you have to purposely put in place. Don't just rely on your own devices to manage this. You can, but you will not be as purposeful with your efforts and as successful with your results as you could potentially be.

One of the best ways to obtain this accountability component is to hire a business coach, even if it is on a yearly or bi-yearly basis. As I mentioned in Chapter Three, I am a true believer in the value of having the right coach to support our efforts in business and in other areas of our lives. As women, we tend to think we can be strong and make it on our own. We can, but we can always "make it" better and faster if we get help along the way.

Hiring a coach is not the only way to have an accountability partner, as we discussed back in Chapter Three. You can also join a mastermind group of like-minded professionals who can support you; or ask a specially selected person to be your accountability partner or business growth mentor. If you decide to join or start a networking group, you can create a subgroup within that chapter of power partners. Assemble people who will support and hold each other accountable for many things as well as your business progression goals.

If you ask people who have achieved great success, they will most likely say they had a defining moment when they made a clear and resolute decision to make a definitive change in their lives. If you don't usually achieve your goals, ask yourself: do you want them enough? Are you comfortable with being uncomfortable?

Whatever the reason, I challenge you to make today the day you decide to do things differently. Believe that whatever you have accomplished so far is only a fraction of what is truly possible for you. You are more powerful, capable, and gifted than you allow yourself to be. The only thing separating you from your grandest vision is belief and the courage to act.

If you don't have urgency, CREATE IT! Determine your *Why* and then leverage that as a powerful motivator for you to accomplish your BEWAGS. Do not wait to be REACTIVE; success lies in being PROACTIVE. Then when the clock strikes midnight on your goal time frame, you will be able to look back to now as the defining moment you began to achieve your Best Year Ever!

CHAPTER 7
Your
Powerful Tribe

In Seth Godin's book, *Tribes* (Portfolio 2008), he shares, *"You can't have a tribe without a leader—and you can't have a leader without a tribe."* Seth does not use the word *manager* or *boss,* because a true leader develops a whole repertoire of skills that are absolutely necessary to guide the people who follow them.

Managers and bosses have employees. Leaders have followers.

Today I learned that:

> *You can't have a tribe without a leader and you can't have a leader without a tribe.*
> — Seth Godin

How Will a Networking Tribe Help You?

You may be questioning whether or not a networking tribe would really be helpful for you and your business. You recognize the need to network to build a strong referral business, but you may be wondering, *why do you need a networking tribe?* Many entrepreneurs and small business professionals think they have to do it all.

It is undeniable that some of the key elements to building a successful business are universal. Regardless of their structure or size, businesses need to accomplish the same thing: they need to attract and keep loyal customers. That may seem easy to achieve, but evidence suggests it's actually getting harder and harder every year to achieve. We are fortunate to be living in an era of advanced technology that is designed to make our lives easier, but with each new tool added to our business tool belt comes a whole new set of challenges and time suckers. Plus, our customers have their own sets of resources that educate them on various options, and may tempt them into the hands of your competitor who may have a shinier and cheaper solution.

This is why we are looking to attract and keep LOYAL customers. Loyal customers, who are willing to turn down a possibly better product or service, or a better price tag in order to keep doing business with you. They know you, they like you, they trust you, and they feel that in the end, you are the best choice.

There are Many Types of Tribes

People have belonged to some sort of tribe or another for millions of years. One of our most powerful survival instincts is to ensure we are connected to other people who will support us while we support them back in return. Since a tribe is simply a group of like-minded people connected to one another by a common interest, it can be easy to see how certain groups may not be recognized as a tribe, and vice versa. We used to live in large and tight-knit families who all lived together or near one another, functioning like a big tribe. All of the family members had a role to play in their tribe and the wise elders usually called the shots. Now, in many cultures, the family has scattered both geographically as well as relationally. We have, in turn, looked toward different avenues to connect with others in meaningful and necessary ways.

Religious Tribes

Perhaps the most well-recognized tribes in our society are those focused around religion. An example could be God as the tribe leader guiding His followers through the Word of the Bible, or it could be Allah through the Quran, or another religious figure, scripture, or leader. Regardless of the differences, religious tribes are similar in that their followers share belief in their leader's vision and in their community as a whole. Drilling down further, we can break the religious tribes down into subtribes. The tribe of Christianity can be broken down into denominations like Catholics, Lutherans, and Baptists, and even further into individual churches where the followers all believe the values of a specific church and its current leader. That is not to say that all church members can be considered tribe members; but the ones who are passionately involved in creating change or accomplishing the church's mission definitely can be.

Sports Tribes

Another type of tribe that is just as widely recognized—yet far less controversial—are the tribes joined by die-hard sports fans. Although I happen to be one of the minority who does not get excited at the beginning of the football season or during the Stanley Cup playoffs (even though I am in Blackhawks territory), I personally know people who get so passionately involved in the evolution of their favorite team that they will do just about anything to follow and support that cause.

In their mind, it is more than just a game or a sporting event; it is their love and their purpose. They live and breathe for their team. They view the other fans as extensions of their family and establish a certain kinship or rivalry with the neighboring fans attending the games with them. There are even websites and apps that will assist fans in finding sports bars and other venues that will be playing their favorite team on their TVs, helping them to commiserate with fellow fans during the game.

Friend and Hobby Tribes

Your group of friends can be considered a tribe because of the dynamics and shared interest of the group. Tribes can develop around a certain philanthropic cause, or among a group of people who share a particular hobby.

Beyond these tribes that flourish through personal face-to-face connections, there are tribes that are created and thrive in the virtual world, with its members communicating through forums and social media channels. These tribes are still able to become strong forces via relationships built over cyberspace. Tribe members make a virtual connection, getting to know the other group members through a headshot photos, profiles and DM's. They share beliefs and have a strong passion for the tribe purpose, believe in the tribe leader and in their tribe community as a whole.

My Harley Tribe

A hobby I enjoy and share with millions of other men and women is riding Harley Davidson motorcycles. I can honestly say that this is more than a hobby for me, and has transitioned into a passion. I am like those die-hard sports fans, but my joy can be found when riding on two wheels with the wind in my hair and my worries left far behind.

I love being a member of my Harley tribe because where ever I am, whatever I am doing, when I am on my bike and I meet a total stranger on another Harley, we will both have an unspoken understanding that we will have each other's backs if needed. Our leader is the Harley brand and we are happy to support and live out what that stands for: personal freedom.

Within the Harley tribe, a subtribe was formed years ago around one particular woman. This woman is the epitome of the rebellious Harley

Davidson biker babe, and she created one of the strongest and most loyal tribes I've ever seen. She started the group with the simple mission of uniting local motorcycle riders, but it's evolved into a strong and expansive community of people who all feel like they are a part of her family. They care about her and support her in many ways. She holds a type of power over them that invokes loyalty that compels her tribe to do just about anything for her. Equally important is that she does not misuse that power.

You can learn more about Ursula Wachowiak in Overcoming Mediocrity Strong Women at www.OvercomingMediocrity.org.

Are you still with me? If so, I'll see you in the next chapter.

CHAPTER 8
Finding and Thriving in Your Tribe

I've given you the basics of joining a networking organization and setting goals, but I know you want to do more than just belong; you want to truly find a tribe and thrive as a result of joining it. This is where you not only join, but flex your leadership muscle in a way that benefits you and your fellow tribe members.

Your Powerful Treasured Tribe

The type of tribe that I want to help you build is the type of tribe I feel all business owners should belong. This is a business tribe that will bring you both financial treasures and relationships that will be treasured for a lifetime. While you don't necessarily need to be the leader of that tribe, you should be an active participant in one way or another. Although the more you put in the more you get out (like most things in life), it is possible to get good results by just being engaged in a tribe without being an active part of the tribe leadership structure.

As I mentioned earlier, just because you're networking, it doesn't mean that you're **Tribe Networking**. Although networking is a part of the equation, tribe networking is far more rewarding. Tribe networking will equip you to get better results and develop richer relationships that will bless you in many ways, and with far less of a time and financial investment on your end. Your new networking tribe will also do more than just generate business for you; the ways you can benefit on other levels from this same group of women could make an almost endless list.

How to Find Your Quality Referral Network

Now that you've decided to focus your future networking efforts with a structured, active and productive referral exchange group, how do you find a good one? You want a networking tribe of your own, but how do you ensure that it will be a productive investment? It's now time to begin shopping and researching the various options.

There are a few national and international organizations with effective structure and policies to ensure the success of their members. They probably started out small like our organization—the Dynamic Professional Women's Network—did, and then grew to become a large and successful resource. There are also smaller groups that have only a few chapters, or maybe only one group, that meets with the same intentions: to refer business to each other. While it's imperative for a referral group to have the correct infrastructure to succeed, the overall success is completely dependent on the members' engagement in the group, as well as the leader's commitment to inspiring the members and leading them through the system.

Do your due diligence when shopping for your new tribe. Don't just settle on a group that has your business category open. Visit the group and interview the leaders, as they should be interviewing you, before deciding on the right group. As you commit, make a decision to invest in the members and in the group as a whole. Don't just visit and make an assumption about the amount of business you will receive from the other members. If you proceed in that way you will surely connect with the wrong group.

You shouldn't be looking for a group that will *give* you business, but instead will *get* you business. That is where the real power lies. You will not know who those women know and can connect you with by meeting them one or two times. You will want to analyze the overall health of the group. Be confident that if the group is operating like a mini successful business, you will have successful networking results when you join that business.

You Found the Golden Goose

Imagine: You found it. After visiting a few referral groups in your area, you found THE group that has it together. It may not necessarily be a large group, because a large group does not always mean a healthy group. But this group is definitely healthy. What's next?

Based on our experience in the Dynamic Professional Women's Network, I suggest that the following three areas of focus and subsequent components be implemented in your group.

If the group you have found is lacking in any of these areas, don't worry. Get connected with the systems they have in place and see how they work. If you feel like their systems could be improved after you have been around a while, ask your chapter leadership team if they would consider implementing some of these suggestions. (Keep in mind that you will have the best results if you make your requests in a way that will not put them on the defensive.) They may not feel like there is a problem with the group or that there is any room for improvement.

Regardless if the whole group shifts their focus—or even if you alone keep the following areas of focus a priority—if you implement these suggestions, you will begin renewing the culture, and other tribe members will follow your example. In the end you will have created a loyal, dynamic and productive referral generating tribe.

1. Building Relationships

The only way to get revenue generating results from your network is to develop strong relationships. It is important to invest in the other members and to get to know them on both a personal and professional level. This doesn't mean you can just show up at your meeting every two weeks and expect miracles. With that strategy you'll get business, but it will only be sporadic and short-lived. For the members of your chapter to become what Bob Burg, author of The Go-Giver, calls your "Personal Walking Ambassadors," you'll need to first become a walking ambassador for them.

2. Building Your Network

You should always focus on adding strategic partners to your referral network. Partners who have the same client base, and could be successful power partner for you or for others. Always invite these potential business partners to future chapter meetings.

- Focus on inviting specific power partners for yourself or others in your group in order to ensure quicker and more abundant referral generation.

- Always have a brochure or flyer available that provides details about your chapter and its meeting schedule. Include your guests on the chapter meeting invitation.

- Send out an e-mail to the members of your chapter introducing your guest prior to their visit (and be sure to copy the guest). This will (1) let the guest know that everyone is looking forward to meeting them (accountability) and (2) help make the guest more comfortable when they arrive at the meeting, because they know that others are expecting them.

- Follow up with every guest, regardless of your perception of them or of their intention to join. Don't feel ashamed to share your interest in them joining your team. If you feel it is not a good fit, a simple "thank you for visiting" message will still make them feel good and important.

3. Training Your Network

Focus your efforts more on training your referral partners than on trying to initiate and close a sale with them. If you want to get extended business from the fellow members of your networking group, it is imperative that you provide them with a clear understanding of your business goals and ideal clients. You want them to operate as if they are an extended sales force for your business, not only a client.

- **Do Not Generalize**

  Be very specific when asking for referrals. Never use the words "anyone," "someone" or "everyone." Most businesses are very diverse, with many different services or products. You can change your request each time to highlight a different need.

- **Maintain the Proper Framework**

  Since you are seeing these new sales associates regularly, it is not the best use of your time to reinforce the same points about your business at every meeting. It is also not a good idea to attempt to give them too much information in such a short period of time. You should attempt to give them one new nugget at each meeting; that nugget should be the current focus so they can look for that specific client. Structure your training to fit into this framework, and end with, "A good lead for me 'today' would be _____."

- **Supporting Materials**

  Arm your members with marketing materials, samples or visual aids that support your weekly focus. You can also regularly share a handout that contains details such as your contact information, your business goals and your current weekly focus. If possible, the card should include an image. This tactic will increase your chances of staying in their minds on a regular basis.

Referral Generation

Perhaps the best way to think about your new referral group is to consider it as your personal marketing/advertisement department and sales team. The group is like a marketing engine which, if not fueled, will stop running. Fuel for your DPWN marketing engine is an ongoing supply of visitors. As visitors come to the chapter, they often become future members, or members' customers. If they do join the chapter, they invariably become a customer of several members, and also bring an abundance of contacts with them to the table.

In short, your chapter must market itself to attract visitors. Marketing your DPWN Chapter should be about more than looking for new members; it's also about looking for new customers for the current members.

In addition to growing the size of your chapter, place equal emphasis on developing the proper skills to ensure the current membership becomes a mega-productive referral machine. The referring power of your members is the single most effective method to increase your membership and your personal marketing exposure.

Systematic Referral by Members

DPWN works because of referrals. That being said, the best way to grow your chapter is also through this word-of-mouth referral process. Each member must take every opportunity to discuss DPWN with other respected business professionals. If your chapter is looking for a particular Power Team Member, start asking around if you don't personally know someone. Your chapter's recruiting efforts and ultimate growth will benefit from referrals more than from ALL OTHER METHODS COMBINED.

Power Partners/Power Teams

Each chapter can be subdivided into smaller subgroups of complimentary and noncompetitive businesses, trades, and professions, called 'Power Partners.' Within each Power Team are many potential specialists who could join the chapter. The ultimate goal is to have a number of Power Teams with six to eight specialists per team. Here's a great way to increase the size of a chapter: have members in each Power Team assume responsibility for increasing the size of their own respective team, thereby increasing the overall chapter membership. Each Power Team is best positioned to decide upon selection criteria for the most suitable candidates to their open categories. (More emphasis will be placed on Power Teams in the next chapter)

What is a QUALIFIED Referral?

While we often have the best intentions and feel like we want to help others in our chapter, we have to be careful only to provide them with the resources they want. While some of your members will be receptive to certain tips that will benefit them or their businesses, most of them will only benefit from qualified referrals.

The difference between a tip, a lead and a referral:

TIP: This is the name of a company or the name of a possible contact. This is more like an idea and will require a cold call to obtain results. Tips may be helpful when opening a new territory or introducing a new product line, but are not what we are looking to exchange with each other in a referral-based group.

LEAD: The contact is considering buying in the near future. They are not actively looking but have taken the member's business card. Permission to call the contact has not been given. Once again, this is not what we are looking to exchange with each other.

REFERRAL: The contact currently seeks a service or product. He or she is a potential buyer. The vendor has been recommended and the buyer wants a call. Call immediately for an appointment! This is our ideal scenario, and what we are focused on generating for each other.

I'll dive deeper into referrals and how to generate and share them in the next chapter.

Why So Many Networking Tribes Fail

When I started my own networking group, I thought it would be such a simple task. All I had to do was find the most amazing business women and invite them to visit our group. I assumed that they would want to join on the spot, because they would see that our network was going to be the best way for them to grow their business.

Fortunately, it didn't turn out that way.

Wait! You may be thinking that you found my first typo, because "did" would seem to make better sense. However, if that had happened, I honestly believe that this initial group would have only lasted a year or so and then fizzled out. You see, I was able to unite a few amazing women right away, who recognized the value of building this new group. But because we were so small, any guest who visited found it hard to see how this budding group of only a few women, could deliver on our promise to generate a strong referral business together.

But that was the blessing in disguise for our little group. We were not going to invite people to join our tribe just because they wanted to gain referrals from us. We needed to strategically recruit women who were going to be focused on learning about each other's businesses so we could, in actuality, become a trained, extended sales force for each other. We needed women who would become invested and committed to each other, and not women who were joining with their hand out and a self-focused mentality. We were looking for visionaries; women who wanted to be a part of our success team.

This is one of the most common reasons why business tribes can have such a short shelf life. It is because they focus on the immediate results and not the overall **big picture** vision. It only took a short time for me to recognize that if we wanted to not only grow this group, but grow it with women who were completely in alignment with our big picture vision, we needed to communicate that overall vision to our guests; not the immediate results. Even if the group grew at a slower pace, it would grow stronger with members who all shared the same vision and values. Thus, it would result in the group adopting a powerful tribe mentality and even more powerful referral generation results.

CHAPTER 9
My
Powerful Tribe

Although I didn't know it at the time, I was soon going to be facing challenges with this first chapter that would equip me to create an strong foundation for a successful women's networking organization. I was dedicating my heart and soul to this group, and as time progressed, I was faced with obstacles I did not foresee. My first big obstacle, although tough, taught me so much about the inner workings of the tribe leadership team.

There are two critical components of a successful tribe:

1. Good leadership is essential to the health of a tribe.

2. The leader needs to be willing to take input and be guided by the tribe, or by a subgroup or leadership team of the tribe. However, it is essential that this team never feels like they are the ones in control of the tribe or of the tribe leader.

I'm not saying that being a tribe leader is hard. But I can assure you that if people join YOUR tribe, they want to be confident in YOU as their tribe leader. When you seek their guidance in a way that allows them to feel like they are in control, the scale can become unbalanced very easily.

They lose their confidence in you, as well as their confidence in the tribe and its ability to complete its mission.

That is exactly what happened with my first tribe. It did not necessarily happen because I neglectfully allowed it, but because I did not recognize that while obtaining guidance from my tribe, I needed to assure them that I was confident and secure in my leadership abilities. They began to think that they, in effect, were able to lead our tribe better than I. However, they did not have any knowledge of the inner workings of the tribe duties that I managed on my own, and they were oblivious to the challenges and the amount of work needed to keep our tribe progressing.

Some women thought that because they helped to make decisions for the tribe, they would be able to lead the tribe more successfully and more effectively than I could. They did not want to be as focused on productivity. They wanted to minimize the rules and be a more casual group. They wanted me to change my vision for the group.

How often do we let our egos get the best of us, only to find it limits our success? This can be the most common and detrimental reason why tribes fail. For a tribe to grow and be healthy, the tribe leader needs to be willing to be humble enough to get input and guidance from its members.

Every process, policy and system created in our organization, although possibly inspired by me, was refined, tweaked, and most importantly, adopted by our leadership team. That process allowed all of the members to become invested in the dynamics of the tribe. It also meant that they took ownership of the tribe's success as well as its failures.

It would have been hard for me to create policies alone and expect the leaders of my chapters to hold their tribe accountable to policies I dictated to them. They needed to have confidence in the effectiveness of our chapter standards. Even if they were not a part of the decision-making process, they knew that the prior leadership team was.

At this point, all sorts of possibilities could be running through your mind about what happened with my tribe: from a mini-coup to an all-out town meeting where I was overthrown and peace was restored. Well, it was actually a little of both. And although it was a bit stressful for me (okay—it was very stressful), I feel it had to happen to make our tribe stronger, and ultimately more desirable to many more professional business women in our area. It also allowed me the opportunity to GROW and THRIVE as a leader.

So, what happened? We actually did have a town meeting of sorts, with our whole group. There was a small cluster of women who wanted to change the structure of our group, in a way that I felt would change our focus and not provide us with productive, referral-generating results.

I felt like they were waging a personal attack on my character, and I immediately got defensive. Unfortunately, it did turn it into a personal attack against me. But I knew that my motives were pure, and the only thing I wanted was to ensure that our group would be beneficial to the members who joined it. That is not to say that I did not welcome input and change. That is exactly what had been happening up until that point: our policies had been developed together as a team. Although there were times that I made solo decisions, I always reviewed the progress with our group and adjusted as needed. Even if I had made a bad decision, I had no problem admitting my mistakes.

Today I learned that:
> *Being challenged in life is inevitable, but being defeated is optional*
> **– Roger Crawford**

So, there we were. Our group had convened to allow myself and my opposition the opportunity to communicate the vision of our tribe and the overall steps we identified to achieve great results together. Not only did I have to bring all of my ideas out of my head and onto paper, I had to be able to communicate them effectively and defend my position successfully.

Standing Up and Speaking Up

As I prepared to state my vision and plan for our referral group, I realized that I needed to put my fears of public speaking behind me. I had just started to believe that God's plan for me was to be in this position, even though it was out of character for my personality and skills at the time. As calmly and clearly as I could, I stood up and stated my vision and plan.

As a result, the chapter split down the middle. Almost half of the women chose to break off into their own group. The remaining women loved the plan I shared with them. They valued their resources, which not only included their financial contributions to the chapter, but their time. They all wanted to invest their time with a group of women who were focused on actively generating business for each other. They knew that the key to the success of our group was for them to build strong relationships with each other, and they wanted to have meetings that were structured and intentional, to bring their businesses to the next level. They also knew it would take work, and were excited to partner with other women who had the same motivation and drive that they did.

Over a decade later, I am happy to say that our group went on to thrive. Meanwhile, the splinter group dwindled away. I think the main reason for our success was that we wanted to keep productivity a priority and we re-built that chapter very strategically. We identified the Power Teams we wanted to build, and we hand-selected women to fill the open positions.

Power Teams

A Power Team is a group of people with complementary professions. They work with the same type of clients and do not compete with each other. The real estate and wedding industries easily provide great examples of Power Teams. A realtor, mortgage broker, insurance agent, stager, and a real estate attorney all service clients looking to purchase property. A wedding planner, photographer, makeup artist and florist are among the many professions that cater to the bride-to-be. When these professions unite to form a power team, and one person in the team gets a new client, they can refer that client to every other member in their team. When you can grasp the idea of what a power team is and how it works, you will understand the importance of it to your business. Power teams are the heart of each DPWN Chapter and the best source of referrals for everyone in the group.

The DPWN Power Team program is designed to enhance the overall productivity of your DPWN chapter while simultaneously create a more intimate and powerful experience within the teams. The chapter size needs to be at least 20 members to be able to form four to six functional sub-groups, but a smaller chapter can be successful if it is committed to expanding rapidly to this size.

Why Power Teams?

What is the benefit of participating in a Power Team if I already meet with these women during my regular DPWN chapter meetings?

- **Bigger Network/More Referrals**
  Undertaking this proactive approach allows the members to better control the results of their networking efforts. It will also result in a more unified chapter as the members work together to find the most complementary and non-competitive businesses to fill up the teams in their chapter.

- **Stronger Network/Better Referrals**
  Within this smaller and more intimate team atmosphere, the members have a better opportunity to gain a deeper understanding, respect, trust and rapport with the other members, thus resulting in decreased time required to generate high quality referrals.

How to Cultivate Power Teams?

Before you can train and encourage the members of your chapter to jump on the Power Team band wagon, you have to begin building your strong team. Make it a priority to begin cultivating Power Partner relationships, and find out as much as possible about your partners so that you can send the right kind of business their way. You need to learn what makes your power team partner special as a person, as well as recognize your partner's ideal prospects.

Step One: Creating the Power Teams

Constitute the Power Teams within your chapter and set the first monthly meeting date at a time separate from the chapter. Set aside 90 minutes for the monthly meeting. At the first Power Team meeting, select a Power Team Coordinator and list all current members on your Suggested Power Team/Hit List Sheet. Identify the other business categories that could join your power team. Select 2–3 categories for each team and prioritize them with a three-star system: 3 stars for the most desirable and 1 star for the lease desirable of the three.

Set up a recruitment strategy to identify candidates for the targeted spots. One honest and powerful script is: "Our DPWN Chapter just created a brand-new power team, and we are looking for a ____. We already have referrals for the right person in the _____ category and I thought of you. We want to fill this spot as quickly as possible..."

You might wish to interview candidates over lunch or a phone call. If they seem interested, and if you and your team are interested in them, invite them to your next chapter meeting. Now you have a qualified prospect for your chapter.

Prospect Criteria – Only recruit the best individuals to team openings if:

a.   They want to build their business (not everyone does!)

b. Their attitude is positive and professional (of course!)

c. They have the capacity to build their business (must be able to service new referrals!)

d. The business category/seat is open in the chapter (one person per profession!)

e. They can offer their product or service in the region (accessible!)

f. They have a depth and breadth of network (they are well-connected in the community!)

g. They have a "farmer" not a "hunter" approach (willing to nurture trusting referral relationships!)

Continue this process until your team has a minimum of five committed members. When new members join, the senior members need to coach and "mentor" the new members along during the first 6 months.

After rounding out the membership of your Power Team, the next step is to begin learning how to generate high quality external referrals for each member within the Power Team. The long-term goal for each power team should be a ratio of three external referrals for every one internal referral.

If one member appears to be struggling, the Power Team should rally. The Power Team Coordinator will be able to focus helpful attention on the member who may be having trouble with some aspect of the program. This Power Team also becomes a marketing focus group to help fine-tune the member's presentations in both infomercial and show case presentations.

CATEGORY LIST

The following list represents various businesses that have benefited from a referral exchange network. As you read through this list, keep in mind that it is not now and will never be complete. It is just meant to spark ideas in your brain about who you can possibly invite into your network.

Category List

Academic/Education

Accountant

Acupuncture

Architect

Art Consultant

Assisted Living

Automotive

Bakery

Bank

Beauty Salon

Bookkeeper

Business Coach

Career Transition

Caterer

Chamber of Commerce

Childcare

Chiropractor

Cleaning Products

Clothing Consultant

Commercial Realtor

Computer Consultant

Construction/Home Improvement

Counselor

Craniosacral Therapy

Credit Card Processing

Credit Consultant

Dance Studio

Day Spa

Dentist

Digital Design & Marketing

Direct Mail Marketing

Dog Training

Editor

Electrical Business

Embroidery Specialist

Employment/Staffing

Energy Consultant

Entertainment

Environmental Wellness

Essential Oils

Esthetician

Etiquette Consultant

Event Coordination

Exercise Coach

Feng Shui Consultant

Financial Advisor

Fire/Flood Restoration

Flooring

Florist

Food Products

Gift Baskets

Gold Buyer

Graphic Designer

Health & Wellness

Health Care Provider

Health Club

Holistic Health

Home Decor

Home Health Agency

Home Inspections

Hospital

Hospitality

Human Resources

HVAC

Hypnotherapy

Image Consultant

Insurance

Interior Design

Jewelry Consultant

Landscape Design

Language Services

Laser Treatments

Legal Professional

Light-Touch Bodywork

Lingerie

Long Term Care Planning

Marketing Consultant

Massage Therapist

Media Consultant

Mortgage Specialist

Nail Salon

Naturopath

Newspaper

Not-for-Profit

Non-Surgical Cosmetic Procedures

Nutritionist

Optometrist

Payroll

Personal Assistant

Pet Care

Pet Products

Photographer

Printer

Private Detective Agency

Professional Cleaning Service

Professional Life Coach

Professional Organizer

Professional Speaker

Promotional Products

Property Management

Property Tax Appeals

Psychotherapist

Publisher

Purification Systems

Purse Consultant

Real Estate Investments

Reflexology

Relocation Service

Resale Shop

Residential Painter

Residential Realtor

Restaurant

Sign Company

Sign Language Professional

Skin Care/Cosmetics

Social Media Expert

Social Service Agency

Speakers Association

Special Event Planner

Spiritual Wellness

Sports & Recreation Center

Stained Glass Artist

Stationer

Technology Consultant

Telecommunications

Title Company

Transportation

Travel Specialist

Tree Specialist

Video Marketing

Virtual Assistant

Water Distribution

Web Designer

Weight Loss & Fitness

Window Treatments

Wine Specialist

Writer/Blogger

Yoga

Who do you know?

Who can you invite into your network from any of the above categories?

Name: Business Category:

_____   _____

_____   _____

_____   _____

_____   _____

_____   _____

_____   _____

_____   _____

_____   _____

_____   _____

_____   _____

_____   _____

CHAPTER 10
Tribe
Insights

We talked earlier about how important it is to properly educate your referral partners so they have insight on your business goals and ideal clients. Don't make the mistake of limiting your potential growth by presenting to your referral team as if your are trying to sell to them.

Yes, it can be important for them to do business with you if the circumstances allow. They need to have an in-depth understanding of your products and/or services, but the real power comes from presenting to your team as if they are your extended sales force. Business partners who are trained to be able to sell for you, not just buy from you. If you don't proceed in this way, everyone will eventually run out of opportunities as time goes on and you've all already worked with each other.

This is where some business networks forget to focus their efforts, and fail to transition to the next level. The real power of your network actually begins at this time. This is when a deep level of trust is established and your partners feel comfortable referring their friends, family, customers and acquaintances to you. This is also when your referral partners have gotten to know you as a person and are willing to invest themselves in your success by actively finding new business for you.

You will leave potential revenue on the table if you do not think and act in this way. If your referral partners don't adequately train you, or take the time and initiative to learn what you feel you need to know to sell for them in return, they too will miss out on potential revenue.

Dynamic Infomercial

When you begin meeting with your partners on a regular basis, it is important that you allot time during your meeting to present your infomercial or elevator pitch. This is critical to the success of your networking tribe… but only if it is executed correctly. We all know how important it is in business to be able to craft and deliver a well-rehearsed elevator pitch. But, when you meet with the same people on a regular basis, it might seem redundant to continue this practice every time you meet; but this is just not the case. First of all, it is important that you've recited that little mini-speech so many times that it becomes second nature for you. What better place to practice this but in a safe and comfortable environment, with other business professionals who are facing similar needs?

Once you have your infomercial down pat, you need to focus on making it dynamic. This means that you now have to make it changeable. You want to always start out with your name and business title. You'll then want to conclude with the statement, "A good referral for me **today** would be _____," and then add your cute and catchy tagline.

Dynamic Infomercial Template

To download this resource, visit
www.ChristieRuffino.com/TT-Resources

Dynamic Info-mercial Worksheet ◆

Introduction (5 seconds)

Smile to your audience, and open with a statement or question that grabs their attention:

_____

_____

About You: Tell them who you are, your position (if relevant) and your company:

_____

Briefly describe your business if needed: _____

Body (13 - 43 seconds)

Focus on ONE specific area of your business to highlight each meeting.

Date _____ - _____

Date _____ - _____

Date _____ - _____

Date _____ - _____

Date _____ - _____

Date _____ - _____

Date _____ - _____

Close (7 seconds)

Name and Company again: _____

Call for Action: A good lead for me TODAY would be... _____

_____

Memory Hook: _____

The main body of your infomercial however, should focus on something different each time. Whether it's your special of the week, a different aspect of your business, a client testimonial, a specific service you offer, etc. You need to use this time to continually educate your tribe partners about your complete business while always triggering ideas in their heads about potential new customers for you.

Referral Follow up

You may think that it should go without saying, but you should immediately take action on every referral given to you. Believe it or not this doesn't always happen. When one of your referral partners, introduces you to a new client opportunity for someone in their database, they are putting their reputation on the line for you. They trust that you will honor that expectation and treat that prospect as if they will become your next best new client. If not, you may jeopardize their relationship together.

It's not only important that you follow up promptly on all referrals you receive, but that you also communicate the outcome of that connection back to the referring member. Keep them in the loop throughout the process with feedback and brief status updates so they will continue to trust you are a good referral partner.

Always appreciate any efforts that are made to generate referrals for you from your referral team. There are many ways to show your appreciation. A simple phone call or a quick e-mail to thank your referees will help to ensure that they continue to come your way. One of the best ways to show your appreciation is a handwritten thank-you card. This will make a far greater impression than a call or e-mail, and keep you in the mind of your referral source longer. I keep a small stack of pre-stamped postcards in my networking bag, as well as on my desk, to make this process very easy and to remind myself of this goal. I also have an action item on my weekly calendar to keep a list of desired recipients and to not forget to send them a nice little note. It takes very little time, yet yields great dividends.

Tribe Success Teams

As you get connected into your tribe, it is important that you also take ownership of the success of your tribe as a whole. This means finding a Success Team position that will add value to the overall health of the group. First, you will need to analyze your strengths, weaknesses, and interests. Then, based on those results and the needs of the group, determine what value you could provide. Schedule time to talk with the tribe leader to figure this out. There should be current positions defined already. If not, work with the leader to create a new position for yourself.

Suggested Action Plan

- Clearly define the current needs of your individual chapter.

- Customize the suggested roles to include your chapter needs.

- Analyze the strengths of your members and individually invite them to participate based on the role in which they would excel.

- Schedule your first success team meeting to discuss the chapter objectives, create the goals, and plan their execution using the Success Team Action Plan.

- Have monthly or quarterly planning meetings to redefine the objectives, goals and execution.

Suggested Success Team Roles

Below is a list of suggested Success Team Roles. We encourage every member of the chapter to take ownership of one or more of these roles. You can modify these roles and create your own roles if desired. Feel free to be creative and have fun with it.

1. Membership Director – External Growth
    a. Run the meeting in the event of the director's absence.
    b. Encourage members to bring guests and develop different ways

to increase membership.

    c. Keep an up-to-date list of categories needed in the group. E-mail that list out regularly.

    d. Greet guests before each meeting. Present an application to every guest and coach them to complete and return to the Chapter Director at the end of the meeting.

    e. Follow-up with each guest after the meeting, and encourage all qualified guests to join and review the potential benefits to them.

2. Membership Director – Internal Growth

    a. Run the meeting in the event of the director's absence.

    b. Work with current members to ensure they are connecting and building relationships with the other members of the chapter.

    c. Work with current members to ensure they are building Power Partnerships and Power Teams.

    d. Work with current members to ensure they are generating and receiving qualified referrals.

3. Secretary

    a. Take meeting notes and send a follow-up recap e-mail.

4. Sergeant of Arms

    a. Set up the meeting tables and display the supplies.

    b. Manage the supply box.

5. One-on-One Coordinator

    a. Manage the One-on-one Connection Session schedule.

6. Education

    a. Cover various networking topics and review DPWN policies.

7. Special Events

    a. Schedule monthly after-hour and other additional chapter events.

    b. Work with other chapters to schedule and promote joint events as determined.

8. Calendar of Networking Events
   a. Compile a list of non-DPWN events to share at the meetings.

9. Greeting Card Coordinator
   a. Send out Birthday, Anniversary or Sympathy cards as needed to the members of the chapter.

10. Philanthropy Chair
    a. Works with the chapter to select and support a not-for-profit organization on a quarterly or yearly basis.

11. Treasurer
    a. Collect lunch money and pay the restaurant prior to the finish of the meeting.
    b. Help ensure that the meals are delivered on time.
    c. Manage money for additional chapter events.

12. Mission Statement/Inspirational Quote
    a. Read the mission statement at the opening of the meeting and read an inspirational quote at the close of the meeting.

13. Marketing
    a. Create chapter marketing items for the members to utilize.

14. Social Networking
    a. Manage a Facebook Fan page and post chapter events.
    b. Actively post chapter meetings on our existing DPWN Meet-up group. DPWN will need to grant administrator access for this person.

15. Guest Hospitality
    a. Welcome and follow up with guests with a friendly note or call.

16. New Member Hospitality
    a. Welcome new members with a friendly all-member note.

17. Mentor
    a. Each chapter member should take on a mentorship role once they have been a member for six months or longer, to help new members get better connected.

18. Librarian
    a. Manage a library for the chapter.

19. Guest Agendas
    a. Prepare updated guest agendas for the meetings for them to follow along with the rest of the group and feel like they belong.

20. Greeters
    a. All Success Team members are encouraged to complete a Greeter training to ensure they are aware of the best way to interact with guests who attend your meetings.

Be Consistent and Dependable

Make certain that you understand and are able to adhere to the attendance requirements of the networking tribe you join, or you will not get the results you desire. Regardless of if the group meets on a weekly, bi-monthly or monthly basis, you have to be dedicated to attending. Regular, consistent attendance and participation demonstrates your dedication to the other members. Inconsistent appearances will be perceived as if you do not value the group and the other members who are showing up as they committed to. It also affects other members; they may be slow to develop loyalty, or they may never develop the full amount of loyalty to you. The power of your networking tribe is centered around the relationships and trust built together, and that cannot be achieved if you do not show up to develop these relationships and support their businesses.

It is also very important that you RSVP to the tribe leader within the time frame they request, or sooner, for two reasons. First, the tribe leader needs to ensure that the venue is set up appropriately for the members and any potential guests. Barring any emergencies, there is no reason why the leader or the venue staff needs to be running around at the last minute with unnecessary changes due to an improper RSVP total. Secondly, many meeting invitation systems, like Evite and Meetup, allow the recipients the ability to see the guests who will be attending the meeting. If the tribe members wait until the last minute to reply to the invitation or neglect to reply at all, the guests may decide to not attend based on the perceived low meeting attendance. Make it a best practice to RSVP "yes" immediately when your meeting invitation is received. You can always go back and modify your response later if something comes up and you can't attend.

Be a Positive Tribe Influencer

Before you walk into your meeting, visualize the best outcome you would like to see transpire. Is it about your guest that plans to join you that day? Is it about the number of referrals you would like to receive? Is it about the excitement that you'll be sharing amazing 3rd party referrals for a few of your sister chapter members?

Whatever the desired outcome, it is easy to trick your brain to believing in what you want to happen. And the more you do this, the easier it will be for these things to actually transpire.

Following is a guided visualization that we use in our community. Feel free to modify it for your individual application.

DPWN Chapter Success Visualization

Close your eyes, breathe in and breathe out, easily and effortlessly.

You drive up to your DPWN meeting place and park the car. You enter the restaurant where you will meet. Feel the anticipation of all the new guests and dynamic sister members that are about to walk in. Stand in the doorway of your meeting area and imagine the space of the meeting room being filled up with energy, enthusiasm and value.

While you're standing there, imagine the number of guests and the possibilities of them joining your fabulous chapter. Come up with a membership number for your chapter. Feel it: how does 15, 20 or even 25 members feel to you? What does a large number of members feel like to you? If it's a little scary, think of the possibilities for the chapter. Reach for the moon and you just might land on the stars.

Feel your measurable membership number for a moment. Tap into a compelling membership number that is obtainable for your chapter. Name it. How will you contribute to that number? Now share it with the rest of your chapter. Spend a few moments with your sister members in discussion; how do you imagine the discussion will go?

You realize the importance of your energy and participation for the success of your chapter and sister members. One by one, members and guests alike begin filling the room. Introductions are flowing from member to guest, and guest to member. Each member and guest has a turn to share their dynamic infomercial, and everyone is encouraging the next member and the next.

Never missing a beat, the rhythm of the meeting flows with informative presenters and business education. Then the time comes for leads and referrals. One at a time, each member stands up and waves a handful of 3rd party referral sheets in the air for each sister member, including you. Leads and referrals… what feels like a good number for you and for the chapter per meeting? Giving 1 lead, 2 leads? Come up with a number that feels like a challenge but doable for you.

You notice the guests paying great attention to the flurry of referrals passed, not to mention the testimonials and thank you's that are filling the room. The leaders count the number of leads and referrals and share it with the dynamic women of the chapter. There is great woo-hooing from everyone—you are surpassing the goals on the DPWN success goal board. The leaders add the number to the goal poster. The guests are in awe.

The members chime in to share the benefits of being part of the DPWN as the guests listen intently. All the while, running through their minds is the message, "I want to be a part of this, a part of these dynamic women. I can contribute to their success and they are the kind of women that will add to my success as well."

How exciting for all the DPWN sisters achieving their goals in a big way! The chapter is growing; every member is receiving the value of friendship, of connection in relationship with each other, of education and great success, being part of the chapter. You realize how important you, as a member, are to the chapter. You are an integral part of what happens in the chapter meetings and as you walk in the world. You are pleased and delighted in your success and all your chapter members' successes.

Pat yourself on the back. You are a great networker; you are part of something spectacular.

When you're ready, come back to the room; eyes open, refreshed and alert.

Negativity is Not Acceptable

Regardless of how good or bad your day or even your week is going, make sure you walk into your chapter meeting with nothing but positive energy. This isn't a group therapy session. Yes! Your tribe is there to support and encourage you when things are tough; but always share your challenges in a more personal setting with select members who are prepared to support you.

If you had a busy week and were not able to make any connections for your team, don't say, "I don't have any referrals this week because…" Instead, focus on something positive like a testimonial, a thank-you for a sister referral partner, or sing praises about a particular connection.

We know that things get crappy now and then, and we know your sister chapter members care about you. But, sharing your challenges need to happen outside of the meeting. On rare occasions, the meeting can be focused on member support; but that needs to be guided by the Chapter Director so it is managed appropriately and so the negative nellies don't continually monopolize the meeting with their perpetual woes.

Communication is Key

The final key to ensure your tribe grows strong, and continues to remain productive, is to have viable and relevant lines of continual communications between the tribe leader and the members.

At one time tribes were strictly a local phenomenon, based on the geographical reach of the available communication channels. It was easy for tribes to gather together and talk in-person to remain strong and effective. Now it's possible to have thriving tribes that span across multiple continents, not just from one village to the next.

While technology continues to evolve, providing newer and more powerful ways to connect, our communication effectiveness does not automatically increase. Now more than ever, it is critical to utilize multiple communication resources to keep your tribe engaged.

Technological advancements are great, but can often lead to our lives becoming busier and more complicated. Our communication avenues need to evolve to adapt with the busyness of each member based on what style works best for them. Technology can often make us feel like we have taken the people out of the equation. It is the tribe leaders' challenge to remain connected to their tribe members on a more personal level. Great leaders create movements by empowering the tribe to communicate.

CHAPTER 11
The Effectiveness of Systems and Resources

In order to give the proper priority to this referral process, it is important to recognize why growing a business through referrals is so vital to its long-term success. It's also important for us to recognize why we *shouldn't* take a passive approach to this process and we *should* put systems and resources in place that will increase our referral generation results.

- Referrals are the cheapest and most time-effective form of customer acquisition — While typical marketing and advertising efforts will provide you with exposure to potential new customers, those efforts are typically costlier, more time consuming and less effective than getting new customers from existing customer referrals.

- Referral prospects are easier to set an appointment with and are easier to close — Prospects introduced to you by a mutual friend or referral source are going to be more receptive to scheduling an appointment with you. These prospects also feel like they already have some sort of a connection to you, which will help them feel like they know, like and trust you.

- Price is less of an issue for referral prospects — The biggest objection most prospects have is often price. While we have to recognize this concern, once you show them that your value far exceeds the price, and that you and the relationship you have already established with this newly-referred client is a large part of this value, the price objection become minimized.

- The process is easily replicable — Your referred clients are more likely to refer additional business to you because that is the model they followed to find you. A referral also builds the loyalty of the person who gave you the referral, so that they will continue to produce more referrals for you.

- Added time — The additional time you'll now have will allow you to spend more time with your family and friends or to allocate towards other areas of your business

With minimal and continual effort, you will be able to reap the many benefits of a thriving referral business.

How to Use Systems to Get Results with Your Intentional Networking

Referrals do not come by accident. They do not come because you have a great product or service. They are the expected result of doing the right things in the referral-gathering process. Systems can be very powerful tools for many applications in life, and even more so in business.

Today I learned that:

Systems permit ordinary people to achieve extraordinary results predictably.
– Michael Gerber

In the Dynamic Professional Women's Network, we've developed processes and systems that, when followed, provide our members with the referral results they desire. I will share a few of these with you so that you can adapt and apply them to cultivate your own referral business.

How to Be Intentional with Your Referral Generation

It is easy to dream of not only getting stacks of referrals at every meeting, but also giving them. The reality, however, is that although you will come across some referral opportunities throughout your daily or weekly activities, you will need to be more intentional with this focus in order to get the necessary results for your referral partners, as well as your own business.

We are all very busy. And it seems like our lives just keep getting busier and busier every day, regardless of the various technological advances designed to make us more efficient and productive.

That being said, it's easy to join a group and show up for the meetings as planned, and then leave to carry on with our business without much thought about our sister members in between the meetings. I can assure you, with minimal efforts like that you will eventually become frustrated with the lack of business you get from the group.

When you are at the meetings, you will be actively connecting with and learning about your referral partners. It will be very natural for you to be excited for them and sincerely wish to help them. The real problem does not lie with your intentions; it lies with your lack of implementation. You will leave the meeting and immediately become immersed back into your

Referral Action Plan

To download this resource, visit
www.ChristieRuffino.com/TT-Resources

own world. The next thing you know, your day is over, then your week is over... and then in two weeks you will be back in your meeting without any opportunities generated during that time away.

Referral Action Plan ◆

Date: _____
DPWN Sister's Name: _____

Best Contact Phone: _____

Best Contact Email: _____
☐ Cell   ☐ EM   ☐ ☐ FB   ☐ LI   ☐ TW   ☐ YLP   ☐ CL

One New Nugget I Learned about My DPWN Sister Today

[   ]

One Aspect I Feel I Would be Most Successful Marketing

[   ]

Connections or Power Partners	Action Taken

Networking Opportunities We Could Attend Together

[   ]

One Way We Could Cross Market/Promote Each Other

[   ]

One-on-One Appointment	Profile Share	LinkedIn Endorsement

My Mission: To become a more engaged & active partner.

For this reason, we've created a few systems that help our members develop best practices with their referral generation efforts. The first of these systems is what we call our Referral Action Plan. It is designed to keep ourselves focused during the in-between times when we are not together.

We use our Referral Action Plan to be more intentional with our efforts to help the sister chapter members who are presenting that day. While you are at the meeting, take time to really listen and reflect on the members who are giving a detailed presentation about their businesses.

Make notes about things like:

- Who could be a great new client for them?

- Who could be a potential new Power Partner?

- Can you create exposure for them in any way on Social Media?

- Are there any events coming up that would benefit them?

- When was the last time you had a one-on-one with them?

- If it's been a while, make a note to get a meeting on your calendars soon!

Write down everything that pops into your head, no matter how insignificant you may think it may be. The reality is that you are going to forget 95% of what you just heard. But, if you take these notes, you will remember more and be better equipped to follow-up in ways that will provide them real value.

Those notes are now your home-work for the next week. Keep them handy! Don't tuck them into your papers to be forgotten. Create a new routine. A non-negotiable follow-up action item for you to support your sister referral partners.

If you really want to grow your business, you really need to be intentional with these efforts, so that you can show up at every meeting proud of how you were able to support the members who presented at the prior meeting. I know it will be a significant investment of your time, but the results will become transformational for your business. When you take consistent actions to provide real value for your tribe, they will be happy to support you when it is your time to present.

It's really all about creating new habits that are focused on them, rather than yourself. This may seem a little counterproductive for you as a small business owner or solopreneur. You may not be used to working as a team or counting on others to help you along. You may also think that you barely have enough time to get your own tasks done, let alone find time to invest in other people's businesses.

Unfortunately, that is the mindset that often sets businesses on a direct path to failure. They do not tap into the powers available to them that are readily used by the "super successful." They do not delegate, they do not outsource, and they definitely do not invest enough time in others, because they are hyper-focused on themselves. These are the signs of an unseasoned business person who has not yet learned how to work efficiently and profitably.

Best Practices

In addition to utilizing our Referral Action Plan, here are some additional best practice activities that should become a routine part of your weekly networking schedule.

1. Every Friday afternoon or Monday morning, review the business cards of each and every one of the members in your chapter and visualize their business. You could create a list, but having that visual tool can be very helpful. I suggest gluing them to a poster board that you can easily update and have handy as needed. You should also create

a reoccurring alarm on your phone to remind you each week of this quick one-minute task.

2. Plot out the meetings you have scheduled for the upcoming week. Visualize any possible connections that could be made for your tribe at upcoming appointments, networking events, personal events, etc. If you don't have any upcoming appointments, schedule a few extra ones with clients or friends that you have been thinking about following up with.

3. When you meet with each client or contact, LISTEN for clues that might suggest that they are looking for a service or product you could help them find. Routinely ask a few probing questions. The more you do this, the more you will be seen as a power connector.

4. Hand out a chapter brochure or concierge list outlining the details of your referral partners' businesses to each client or contact you meet. Indicate that this is your preferred list of service providers and vendors that you recommend highly. Only include those that you know well and are confident in the quality of their work.

5. If you discover that your client or contact is interested in someone on your preferred list, ask them for permission for your referral partner to contact them about their needs. Don't just give them the list and expect them to follow up. Give your referral partner control of their potential business opportunity.

6. If there don't seem to be any obvious connections to be made for your referral partners, don't feel embarrassed to ask for a referral. Explain that you've had the most success at building your business through referrals, and that you've developed a list of preferred vendors you would be willing to introduce them to if they should have any future needs. Just plant the seed. Follow up with a concierge list or a link to a business partner page on your website, if available. You could

even create a referral program that provides discounts or benefits from your referral partners.

Remember that quality beats quantity every time. Be sure that the referrals you generate are for potential buyers who are looking to make a transaction in the immediate future. Always include detailed contact information and ask for permission to make the connection so that your referral partner has the power to contact that new potential client.

Be sure to follow up on the referrals you give to ensure that a great connection was made and no further help is needed. If you use referral tracking forms with your network, keep them handy at all times as a constant reminder to create and maintain good referral habits.

Our Goal is to Purposefully Look for Qualified Referrals for Our Tribe.

Although we will naturally begin doing business with our referral partners, that is not our primary objective. It is beneficial to become a customer, when possible, to get to know their products and/or services, so you can be confidently and knowledgably referring customers to them. However, that needs to be only the beginning of the process. Our actions must support our goal to generate referrals by making introductions with friends and acquaintances who would be great potential clients. Take the time to learn what their ideal clients would look like so you are not generating meaningless connections for them.

Hold regular Connection Sessions or one-on-one meetings with your partners over coffee/tea or lunch to get to know more about them. This is one of the best ways to develop deep personal relationships with each other. After that initial meeting, follow-up meetings should continue throughout the year to learn more about each other's businesses and to maintain the already-established bond.

If you are not sure about how to support one of your referral partners at any time, a good question to ask them would be: "How will I know if someone I am speaking with (this week) would be a good prospect for you?"

It is important that you do not sit back and wait for opportunities to present themselves. You need to purposefully and actively look for opportunities to generate third party/external referrals for them. Make sure you are providing support for the whole team. There will always be some businesses that are harder to provide frequent qualified referrals because of the nature of the business, but don't let that be an excuse to stop actively trying on a consistent basis.

How to Give QUALIFIED Referrals

"Giving" referrals should take priority over "getting" referrals if you want to have a healthy and productive referral-generating network. It is only after we focus on others' success that we will truly reap the benefit of growing our own business through referrals.

One of the most impactful books that I have had the pleasure of reading is The Go-Giver by Bob Burg and John David Mann. Although I have read this book several times over the years, my first exposure to this little gem was during the first year of establishing DPWN. Before reading this book, I had naturally been inclined to helping others, but I never really thought about the rewards that I received in return for engaging with others in this manner. I viewed the whole matter as a 50/50 give-and-take process. How wrong could I be?

The Go-Giver is a short parable about one man's journey to discover the power of giving. Through a series of events and interactions with other givers, he learns how to transform his business and, ultimately, his life in a direction that ends up being far more rewarding than he could have ever imagined. He learns the power of the "five laws of stratospheric success."

Five Laws of Stratospheric Success

1. The Law of Value — Your true worth is determined by how much more you give in value than you take in payment.

2. The Law of Compensation — Your income is determined by how many people you serve and how well you serve them.

3. The Law of Influence — Your influence is determined by how abundantly you place other people's interests first.

4. The Law of Authenticity — The most valuable gift you have to offer is yourself.

5. The Law of Receptivity — The key to effective giving is to stay open to receiving.

The more you provide authentic support for your tribe partners, the more business you will eventually get back in return. That does not mean that your efforts are intended to be manipulative or self-serving. You have to be sincere with your motivations to help.

As Bob Burg shares in this bestselling book, "You give because you love to. It's not a strategy, it's a way of life and when you do, then very profitable things begin to happen."

Referral Generation Results

Over time, you will create strong relationships with your referral team.

Referral Tracking Chart

To download this resource, visit
www.ChristieRuffino.com/TT-Resources

Member Name: _____

Business Category: _____

Membership Date: _____ Website Password: _____

Referral Tracking Chart

Jan-March							TOTAL
Inside Given							
Outside Given							
Inside Received							
Outside Received							
Your Guests							
Your New Members							

April-June							TOTAL
Inside Given							
Outside Given							
Inside Received							
Outside Received							
Your Guests							
Your New Members							

July - September							TOTAL
Inside Given							
Outside Given							
Inside Received							
Outside Received							
Your Guests							
Your New Members							

October - December							TOTAL
Inside Given							
Outside Given							
Inside Received							
Outside Received							
Your Guests							
Your New Members							

And if you are in a women's only group, your relationships will most likely develop into a strong sisterhood. Not only will you be on a business journey together, you will be on a life journey as well.

These dynamics can lead to a very strong referral team… or they could possibly become the demise of the team. Once we become friends, it is easy to become lax on productivity. We become comfortable with each other and our focus shifts to become more relational. For that reason, we need to remain focused on the results we are creating together in the group.

Each quarter, the core leadership team of the group should meet to determine the productivity goals they want to achieve with membership growth, as well as the 3rd party referral generation growth. They should track the progress of the group and ensure that each goal is set based on the overall progress of the group throughout past quarters or years.

As a member, it is also important that you are tracking your results as well. We've created a Referral Tracking Chart for our members to use every year to gauge the progress they are making in the group. We can't stay in a group that is not serving us, and we can't stay in a group if we are not serving others.

I'm not saying that anyone should make a decision to hastily jump into a new group. My thought process is that 90% of the time, if you feel that your group is weak, you have the power to make it stronger again. Be a part of the solution. Get involved with the leadership team to help implement strategies that will create the desired results; strategies that are proven to work. There is no need to re-create the wheel and make change difficult. Our library of resources provides the tools and the step-by-step plans to help a referral group increase their referral generation results with teamwork, accountability, strong leadership and enhanced relationships.

You can learn more about our community at www.OurDPWN.com

AFTERWORD

We need each other.

We all bring different characteristics to the table as entrepreneurs and business professionals; characteristics that make us better in some areas and just plain stinky in others.

While I never intended to start a networking organization, God started me down a path that would utilize a variety of my strengths to create a thriving referral generation community for women. And then, because I wanted more women to reap the same benefits our first group was experiencing, I went on to create systems for others to replicate our success.

Systems which, if utilized, will allow other professional women to create their own tribes of business referral partners.

One of my biggest joys now is being asked to visit one of our chapters to meet new members, catch up with seasoned members, and greet any visiting guests. Regardless of the location and history of that chapter, I always see a common thread among the long-term members.

- They found us because they were looking to increase their referral business.

- They joined us because they saw how productive our group was for the members, and they wanted similar results for themselves.

- They stayed with us because they built strong relationships with the women in their group who over time become their mentors, advisors, accountability partners, treasured friends and so much more.

They discovered that we were more than just another networking group. They saw how we had created a culture of women who value the go-give philosophy and who are committed to each other and to each other's success.

We invite you to join our DPWN Community at www.OurDPWN.com.

If there is not a DPWN Chapter in your area, start one. We have a proven system and we provide the training and resources to make the adventure easy and fun.

If you're not a natural leader and don't want to take that on, find a similar type of referral group in your area. Get plugged in and adopt our best-practices into that group to increase its productivity.

Either way, "nothing changes if nothing changes." So, if you are looking to increase your client base through referrals, it is up to you to execute the best plan to make that happen.

More Business Building Resources

To download all of the resources in this book and more, visit
www.ChristieRuffino.com/TT-Resources

TREASURED
TRIBES

DPWN

Dynamic Professional
Women's Network

www.OurDPWN.com

WHAT IS YOUR STORY?

Every year, we feature twenty-plus women in our Overcoming Mediocrity series of books. These women fearlessly and transparently share their stories of encouragement, inspiration and prosperity.

They are not fashion models or award-winning writers. They're simply amazing individuals who made the decision to share their stories to light the way for others to also see their own inner brilliance.

If you're ready to share your story with some valuable tips and resources; and you'd love to become an Amazon Bestselling author, but don't have the time, money or audience to make it happen right now, this project is the perfect fit for you.

Visit www.OvercomingMediocrity.org to check out the project details and then let's book a call to talk about YOUR story.

You can also find the whole series of books on Amazon.

Christie Ruffino

DPWN President/Founder

NOTES

www.ingramcontent.com/pod-product-compliance
Lightning Source LLC
Chambersburg PA
CBHW050509210326
41521CB00011B/2386